Lived To Tell

A Celebration of Friends Lost to AIDS

A MEMOIR

D. Dave Churchill

Lived to Tell: A Celebration Of Friends Lost To AIDS

Copyright © 2024 David Churchill (writing under the nom de plume D. Dave Churchill.)

This book is memoir [or based on true events]. It reflects the author's present recollections of experiences over time. Some names and characteristics may have been changed, some events may have been compressed, and some dialogue may have been recreated.

The author has tried to recreate events, locales and conversations from his memories of them. This memoir is a truthful recollection of actual events in the author's life and contains explicit language and explicit sexual content and adult themes. The contents of this book are suitable only for mature audiences.

All rights reserved. No part of this publication may be reproduced, distributed, or transmitted in any form or by any means, including photocopying, recording, or other means..

Publishing Date: 02/15/2025

For

KRIS KAMM

Probably. Still. Forever.

Lived to Tell

We have been gay
Going our way
Life has been beautiful
We have been young

~ Oscar Hammerstein II & Sigmund Romberg
When I Grow Too Old to Dream

Acknowledgements

I would like to thank Stuart at The AIDS Memorial on Instagram for posting my first remembrance of a friend. Also, his 295K followers, some of whom suggested I write a book. If this book touched you in any way, please consider following his account.

I would like to thank those fellow writers who helped me see myself as a writer: Jonathan Kieran; Steve Cubine; Steven Price; Tracy McCubbin; John D'Ignacio and Treena Orchard. Your appreciation of a particular turn of phrase buoyed me and kept me afloat through these five long years. If you enjoy good writing find them on Amazon.

My faithful blog readers who stuck with me as I learned how to write: David Primuth, a coworker at my first real job; Ellen Parker a friend from the early 1990's; Analisa Krol, Jason's mom; a grade school sweetheart, Eileen Lepionka; and an old flame, Ben Simon. Your frequent comments kept me going.

And to those whose generous financial support kept the wolves from the door while I devoted myself to this book: Rob Parker (Bucky from Laguna Days), Ewa Marchiondo, Donna Coupe & Christina Plank, and Ben Simon.

To all those who contributed to my Kickstarter and GoFundMe pleas: Christine Capello, Rachel Ogulnick, Sarah Thomas, Efie Protopappas, David Fitzgerald-Crosby, Marnee Weber, Sira Hotsinpiller, Ronnie Todd, Toni Crummett, Chuck Greenberg, William W. Hopper, Jeanne Jackson, Mikie Doctor, Aaron Doctor, Emily Green, Steven Cohen, Monika Travis, Gary Whitfield, Peter Isacksen, Leora Langs, Hanna Dasenbrock, Linda Sullivan, Todd Cochran, Todd Sievers, Denise Della Valle, Treena Orchard, Ron Culves, Scott Hawkins, Eric Gold, Kathleen McGivney, Beth Brook-Moir, Bryan Greiner and all the anonymous donors.

And to those old friends who checked in on me and helped me get by until my next Social Security Check: Scott Harper, Kris Kamm, Jackie Cohen, Julie Campau Miller, Sean Travis and Ellen Parker.

To the surviving Beach House Boys who kept me in their thoughts and gave me money for new tires; Scott Elliott and his husband, James Crank; Mark Jenssen; and Kevin Clew who gave me a safe haven to park my Airstream during COVID.

Special thanks to Scott Harper a design genius who gifted me with this beautiful cover. Gratitude to Kristen Heimerl who sent copywriting gigs my way, and who offered to help market this book, thanks, Toni! And to Amy Eller who helped me over the hurdle.

Special thanks to Eric and Jenifer Metz who welcomed and befriended the long-haired stranger from California who rolled into Florida in a trailer. Your surprise trips and company kept me going. And to Dylan Metz who kept my computer going.

I must remember my deceased mom, who instilled in me the belief that I could do or be anything (except be gay). To my Godmother Pat Harlacher who inscribed a thesaurus "To the Pulitzer Prize Winner," back in 1980. And my Dad, from whom I inherited my love of telling a good story.

Eternal gratitude to Jacqueline Neumeier who helped me start a new life in Manhattan Beach. To Joe and Jen Agliozzo who accepted me and gave me a place to hide and heal on the 36th Street volleyball courts. And to the 36th Street crew, both old and new who gave me sport and friendship.

To the devoted care team who made it possible for me to recover from 2 back-to-back strokes: Kris Kamm; Jackie Cohen; Michelle Ricker; Hunter Kamm and Tanner Delk. Also to Umberto and Babette who kept me on payroll. And to T. Max Maxwell who treated me like nothing had changed. And J.D. Ciasulli who taught me to Cowboy Up on my first post recovery trip to Las Vegas.

I'd like to single out Myles Guidry, a reader whom I have never met, who always surprised me with money for a daiquiri when I needed it the most, after a week of living in the past.

A big thank you to all the bartenders who make a perfect Daiquiri: John at Charthouse who won't give me his last name, but did give me my nickname of Daiquiri Dave. And the other Charthouse crew: Matt, Cory, Brandan;, and the valet parkers Mac, Yuri and the tall ginger whose name I am blanking on. Shelly Chavarria at Florida Fresh, and Lea. Ethan Tyler at Lourdes Library and Meredith and Julee Jules and Jimena; Ian at Iron Oak Post; Jake and Ashley Spann and Alec Fletcher wherever they are now; Cassaundra Fornier at Hemingways, plus Alyssa, Allie and Tyler; Lauren Gibson and all the young folks who put up with me at Alibi: Cory, Darrius, Jordan, Emma, Katya, Marisha, Maria, Gabby, Corby and Erin. Each of these young people gave me a friendly smile and a stiff drink when I needed one after a long day of wrestling with ghosts. They lent me an ear and put up with my behaving like it was still 1980, misbehaving as if I were still their age. They kept me connected to the world of the living.

    Finally, thanks to all the caregivers who showed unbelievable courage in those dark days- the doctors, nurses, activists, loved ones and strangers who eased the pain and fear of the dying.

    This book is dedicated to all the survivors.

    ~ Daquiri Dave Churchill

Lived to Tell

Table of Contents

1	And Then There Was One
2	Duff Paddock
3	Seasons In The Sun
4	This Town
5	West Street Beach 1979
6	Michael Rotella
7	Get Your Kicks On Route 66
8	Take It On The Run
9	Dean Frey
10	Is That All There Is?
11	Looking For Love In All The Wrong Places
12	Get Down Tonight
13	Turn The Beat Around
14	Magic
15	Galveston, Oh Galveston
16	Donnie McPhedran
17	Southern Nights
18	More, More, More
19	When The Saints Go Marching In
20	Last Chance Texaco
21	Disco Inferno
22	Maniac
23	Hanging On The Telephone
24	Love Is A Stranger
25	Stop Your Sobbing
26	Hal Story
27	We Are Family
28	Larry Lane
29	Afternoon Delight
30	Autumn Changes
31	Bo Frieden
32	Joseph Genna
33	Juan Cruz
34	New Kid In Town
35	Fade Away And Radiate
36	I Will Survive

And Then There Was One | CHAPTER 1

I am the only survivor from this picture. I am the leggy blonde on the far right. These boys were my chosen family. I remember this night as if it were yesterday. This was the beginning of Memorial Day weekend in 1981. Each of these boys was lost to AIDS before the decade was done

We met and made a home in Laguna Beach, California. Laguna was an odd artist's colony, with storybook homes cascading down the hillside towards the ocean. One year, some of these homes slid into the ocean. Back then, it was an enchanted kingdom. The undeveloped Irvine Ranch surrounded the hamlet like a moat. For miles, you drove past grazing cows and roadside fruit stands.

Laguna was isolated from conservative Orange County. Jagged cliffs stood sentry o'er the sand. Hidden coves dotted the coastline, each a private oasis for locals only. Although Laguna was a tourist town, there was only one public beach. Main Beach was the only beach visible from the Coast Highway. It lay at the mouth of Laguna Canyon Road.

Harder to find was a clandestine beach, known only to the world's homosexuals. Bookended by Camel Point and Table Rock in South Laguna, West Street Beach was a secluded, crescent-shaped cove. Like a secret garden it was accessible only by a flagstone path obscured by Eucalyptus and Bougainvillea. This used to be our playground. From the top of the cliffs, it resembled a Mondrian painting every inch of sand was covered with colorful beach towels. A handful of sailing yachts bobbed in the cerulean cove. Aboard these, rich gay men entertained minor titles visiting between seasons in Mykonos and Fire Island, On any given day there were at least a thousand men sunning on the sand of this unforgettable beach. We were the undisputed kings of the beach.

Each of us had run away from an unwelcoming home. We were like the Lost Boys from *Peter Pan*.

The seaside town of Laguna Beach was our Neverland. A remnant of the hippie's Summer of Love in 1967, one could still get a free meal at the Hare Krishna Centre on Glenneyre St. on Monday nights.

We never needed that free meal. Without fail, the six of us were always invited to a dinner party.

Parties were thrown in Laguna on any given night at the end of the 1970's, The homosexual residents were celebrating the freedoms earned after Stonewall. Like in the *Great Gatsby*, you didn't need an invitation. *The doors were open to anyone who came for the party with a simplicity of heart, which was its own ticket of admission.* Like Gatsby's, these parties were overflowing with food and drink.

Throughout that first year, we never once had to make a meal. I remember one party at a new home on Top of the World (locals referred to this hillside development as the "Swish Alps" because the majority of residents was gay).

According to our friend Steven Henderson, that night a condo developer from Miami removed the mirrored door from the wardrobe, laid it flat on the bed and wrote "Surrender Dorothy," in cocaine. After this, the Gatsby's of Laguna no longer sprung for a caterer.

This is a snapshot that was taken at one of those grand soirees. We are in an anteroom in Jim Moniz' home at 1515 Emerald Bay.

Upstairs Calvin Klein and David Geffen are holding court while Kevin Gill and Bradley Cain feign rapt attention. Rob Parker and John Brandon melt on Quaaludes into the dove gray silk furniture.

Our cohort taking this picture is Stevie B, Jim's latest boy toy. Stevie B. has liberated a vial of coke, we escaped the old people and have holed up outside in what must have been the pool house. On the far left is Donnie McPhedran, next to him is a trick he picked up on the beach, John from Santa Barbara. To his right is the callipygian Duff Paddock of the pale green eyes and devastating charm. Duff is possessively wrapped around his new boyfriend, Dean Frey, fresh out of Ronald Reagan's neighborhood of Pacific Palisades. Next to them was an actor I was besotted with,

Rob Kreuger, this was only to be our second date. I knew as the flashcube popped that Rob had bigger fish to fry.

One by one, AIDS took each of these young men in the prime of their life. Somehow, I lived to tell. This is the story of my Lost Friends.

Although I am not certain how their last days played out, I do know how this night ended.

With Duff's encouragement we stripped bare-assed naked and wrapped ourselves in plush bath sheets and smeared cold cream on our faces to recreate the iconic album cover of the Go Go's *Beauty and the Beat*.

Checking up on his kept boy, Jim Moniz led a conga line of bold face names down the stairs to spy on Stevie B. And there they found the trophy twinks of Laguna Beach dressed as Valley Girls. Mortified, we jumped in the pool, rubbed off the cold cream and abandoned our towels. We emerged from the pool flaunting our assets. We were the volleyball gods of West Street Beach, goddammit. So ashamed to be caught camping it up, we agreed that we had to leave town. Within a week we left for a cross-country road trip in my convertible, six boys in a Camaro for two months.

This is a remembrance of my Lost Friends, these Peter Pans who never had the chance to grow up.

Duff Paddock | CHAPTER 2

Duff Paddock was my first gay friend. Forty years later I don't remember how we met. Duff was the most beautiful boy I had ever seen. He had alabaster skin slightly burnished by the sun. Like rouge, the sunburn only served to highlight his cheekbones and emphasize the muscular curves of his shoulders and chest. Under a thicket of glossy black hair, the first thing you noticed was his startling green eyes.

The first thing that I noticed was the creamy curves of his buttocks thrusting above of his low-slung boardshorts, "You could bounce a quarter off that ass," somebody was always muttering whenever he would pass by.

Although I don't recall how we met, I am certain I tried to pick him up on the gay beach in Laguna.

Newly arrived in California, I spent a year searching for the gay beach. Most of the best beaches in Laguna were hidden coves known only to locals. they were only accessible through unmarked cutoffs through the brush.

I spent the whole of 1978 inquiring at the gay beach in Long Beach, "Does anyone know how to find the gay beach in Laguna?" only to be met with come-ons like, " No reason to drive to Laguna, I've got all the meat you need right here."

"Sonny, let me take you there and show you in person."

"You can drive my Corvette."

Because I had my own Camaro, I would drive it down Pacific Coast Highway and attempt to find this beach myself.

I ended up timidly asking beachgoers on Laguna's Main Beach, "Do you know how to find West Street Beach?"

In 1978, this question was generally answered with, "Beat it, Fucking Faggot."

Eventually I found it by happenstance. One day I woke up on it.

I had met a boy at the Odyssey 1 Disco on Beverly Blvd. in Hollywood. Because he still lived with his parents, he suggested we go to the beach. We had split a Disco Biscuit, better known as a Quaalude. This Quaalude explains why I was just waking up as the early beachgoers were arriving. I could hear their hoots and hollers as they staked out territory on the sand. My eyes were glued shut by a combination of sleep and sand. I tossed off the beach towel I was using as a blanket and quickly dove into the ocean to wake myself up.

Upon opening my eyes, I saw that this was the paradise I had been dreaming about. Already hundreds of boys my age were frolicking on the beach, playing Kadima, tossing a Frisbee and tiptoeing into the surf. These boys were the picture of health and vitality, unlike the leathered lotharios that populated the gay beach in Long Beach. I had finally found my tribe.

At 19, I was still trying to find my place in the world. I had spent too many years denying my identity, now I was trying to create one. I quickly grabbed my beach towel and abandoned the sleeping boy without waking him. He reminded me too much of the boy I no longer wanted to be. Surreptitiously I moved to a spot among the prettiest boys on the beach.

This is where I must have met Duff Paddock.

"Want to swim out to my friend's boat?" Duff asked.

Calculating whether this was a challenge to test my masculinity, I chose to answer "Yes!"

I noticed that the tiny cove between two rock outcroppings had been filled with sailboats since I first woke up. On each sailboat were about a dozen men disco dancing, half-naked except for tiny speedos. Like me, Duff wore surfboarding trunks. We stood shoulder to shoulder at the edge of the surf, looking out at the white boats bobbing in the dark indigo water, waiting for the right time to enter the ocean.

West Street Beach had a deadly shore break. Head high waves would crash right at the tideline. As we stood there, a giant wave hit and washed out all the body-builders standing (posing) around us, they were scattered like Styrofoam cups, rolling in the surf, screaming and squealing. Duff grabbed my hand, we ran into the water and dove under the next wave before it hit the shore.

Duff had a powerful stroke, he did the Australian Crawl.

Before I got halfway out, he was already climbing aboard a yacht. The Pacific Ocean was ice cold. I was on my back treading water trying to locate the boat Duff got on. I was not a swimmer. I had been excused from swim class in Pennsylvania due to a chlorine allergy.

Soon Duff was hanging off a boat calling to me, "Hey, Blondie, over here!" He'd obviously forgotten my name. which didn't bode well for my romantic fantasy.

Exhausted, I hoisted myself up onto the boat deck, and immediately collapsed. I spread my lanky body against the warmth of the boat's deck to shake off the chill from the ocean. By the appreciative glances, I was aware my wet, tan body looked desirable against the white of the boat's deck.

Duff had knelt next to me and said, "I want you to meet my friend Terry Causey. This is his boat."

I got up on unsteady feet and was offered a flute of champagne. In the darkness of the cabin cruiser's salon, Terry Causey was cutting lines of cocaine on a mirror, as Duff slid into the banquette next to him. I excused myself, at this point I was adamant that I did not do drugs. In my thinking, Quaaludes were exempt as they were prescription. So, I took the one that was offered to me as a parting gift. With champagne in hand, I steadied myself against the buffet as the boat bobbed in the ocean.

"Try the caviar," said the stranger whose hairy chest was pressed against my back.

I tried the only food that I recognized. I took a shrimp. It was all I could manage with a flute of champagne in my other hand. I broke away from the man pressed against me and back onto the warm, sunny deck. I gazed over the low railing at the beach I had just discovered. From this vantage point it seemed that the size of the crowd had doubled since I got on this boat. It appeared that every inch of sand was taken.

There was a volleyball game going on at the foot of the cliffs, I could see the ball bouncing high in the air. The court appeared to be near where I left my towel. Behind the volleyball court a lush green lawn ran up the hillside to a grand white Spanish hacienda at the top of the cliff. In the decade I spent on this beach, I never noticed an occupant in that house. I saw people in the other more modern homes perched on the cliffs, but none of them had lawns or access to the beach.

There was only one path to the beach, it was an emergency access road for a lifeguard Jeep. I remember the summer an ambulance used it to take a bodybuilder friend of Bucky's to the ER. His chest was so overdeveloped that we nicknamed him Jayne (as in Mansfield).

From the boat, the beachgoers still arriving looked like a trail of ants coming down to the beach.

One lone ant was heading back up the hill. I thought he could have been the boy I spent the night with. From the boat, the spot where we had camped looked deserted. The tide had already washed away the pillows we had made in the sand. I had assumed that Duff had abandoned me like I did that boy. I prepared to dive off the yacht and swim back to shore, alone.

"You better use the head, before you head back to the beach." Someone said behind me. "There are no restrooms on that beach."

The groping hand made me realize I should skip the head.

"Thanks, but I'll just pee in the ocean," I said.

"Eeew," a new voice said. "Are you into that kinky stuff?"

It was Duff suddenly tossed against me as the boat rocked.

"Duff, do you think we're going to hit those rocks?" I pointed to deadly rocks jutting up out of the ocean just yards from the bow of the boat.

"Holy shit!" his eyes widened. "I'll race you to shore."

His dive took him several yards to shore. I was still looking for a spot to set my champagne flute. "Here," I handed it to the hand that was approaching my ass.

Instead of diving I jumped into the ocean and promptly sunk to the rocky bottom. I desperately clawed my way to the surface only to hit my head on the bottom of the yacht. Maybe it wasn't a good idea to swim on a Quaalude. The boat's two propellers kicked on and I dove down and out of their way and finally came up for air.

"Are you OK?" Duff asked just a few yards away.

Re-oriented I did a back stroke towards the shore. Duff had beat me but he was bobbing in the water waiting for the waves to stop breaking.

"Last one in is a rotten egg!" I shouted, and body surfed the next wave in.

With this shore break, I could have broken my neck. Which is the reason the ambulance once came for Bucky's friend Jayne. Duff stumbles onto the shore and clings to me like Deborah Kerr to Burt Lancaster.

"That one knocked the wind outta me," Duff coughed.

Luckily for me, a big coke booger swinging over his lips stopped me from trying to kiss him.

As he broke away, he asked, "Want to give me a ride home?"

Seasons in the Sun | CHAPTER 3

This is what I thought Duff asked, "Want to take me home?" The blue sky, the bronzed bodies and the blazing sun led me to believe I was in a Technicolor Douglas Sirk romance. That was the dialogue I wanted to hear.

All eyes were on Duff as he made his way back to his towel. We were dripping wet from our swim from the boat. I felt like Jane Russell walking beside Marilyn Monroe through the ship's dining room in *Gentlemen Prefer Blondes*.

This is when I first heard, "You can bounce a quarter off that ass."

"Look at the legs on the new friend," looking over my shoulder I saw a well-built black man gazing at me.

I would later come to know him as George Smith. I grabbed my beach towel, wrapped it around my wet trunks and sat beside Duff, so close I could feel the heat of his sunburned shoulders. Duff began introducing me to the circle of friends that surrounded him.

"I'm Dave Churchill," I said realizing Duff still couldn't remember my name.

They perfunctorily shook my hand as they continued to gaze at Duff.

"We've got to go," Duff said to their disappointment. "Can you still give me a ride?" Duff asked.

"Sure," I was thrilled that his friends were jealous of me. I realized I was nothing but his taxi.

"I've got to settle up with my maid." He said grandly, by way of goodbye. "Do you have to say goodbye to anyone?" Duff asked me.

I briefly thought of the boy I had just spent the night with. I remembered, with gooseflesh rising on my arms, that he had driven his own car. "No. I'm by myself."

Shuddering, I turned to stare into the bright sun to erase the image from the night before. As I followed my trick into Laguna, I watched that boy sideswipe four cars along Laguna Canyon Road.

I soon forgot the dangers of driving on Ludes as I basked in the limelight of following Duff Paddock. Zig-zagging on the hot sand, through the adoring crowd. As if following Duff's lead, a majority of the crowd got up to leave the beach. I assumed since the star had left the stage, the fans believed the show was over. In later years I learned that these were the young men that had to get to jobs as waiters in restaurants. I felt sorry for them having to leave the beach before 4:00 in the afternoon.

Leading the parade up the hill, I had to hop as the asphalt burned my bare feet. I left Duff's side to find a patch of cool shade to walk on.

"You'll adore Cory." Duff said from the sunny side of the street.

I couldn't hear the rest of what he said. He was too far away, and the sound of the crashing waves drowned out his voice.

I was crestfallen, wondering if this Cory was his lover.

Before the top of the fire road, Duff crossed over in front of me to a hidden path cut through the hedge between two houses. In the shade, the cool flagstone soothed my burning feet.

"I'm afraid we're going to miss her." I heard Duff continue his conversation now that we were again side by side.

I turned and took one last look at the crescent of beach. White sails were being raised on the remaining sailboats, as half-naked men dove into the water to head back to the beach.

"Hurry Up!" Duff called.

This was my first red flag, Duff could be bossy. I took one last look at this hidden paradise, trying to remember where this path could be found. We emerged through a cut out arch in the hedge, directly onto Pacific Coast Highway. Speeding cars were thundering past us, zooming up the hill and around the curve where we exited.

"Faggots!" Someone spit as they passed by in a Datsun pickup.

My green convertible Camaro was the first car parked near the arch in the hedge. I unlocked the passenger door for Duff, who quickly rolled down his window to let the ocean breeze into the sweltering car. I timidly opened my drivers' door into oncoming traffic. I started the car and powered down the convertible top. I revved the rumbling V8 to get the attention of two young gay boys walking past us.

I wanted everyone to see I was leaving with Duff Paddock.

Before the internet, we joked that the most effective way to spread gossip was, "Telephone, Telegraph, or Tell a queer."

I whipped a U-turn across 4 lanes of speeding traffic on the Coast Highway and headed back into Laguna proper. A Donna Summer 8-track was in the Alpine stereo. Duff sang along to *Heaven Knows*. In the four years Duff was my best friend, I only recall him singing twice. The second time we sang was on a balcony perched over a canyon in his newly leased home on Sunset Plaza in the Hollywood Hills. Like two old show queens, we belted *Memory* from *Cats*.

"I can dream of the old days, Life was beautiful then. I remember the time I knew what happiness was." Only 26, we understood these lyrics.

People we knew were beginning to die.

Driving up the Coast Highway with the wind in our hair, this was our, *"life was beautiful then."*

As we passed Thalia Street Surf Shop, Duff pointed, "Just past that gas station," he said, "park in front of the Bead Shop."

Ten years later, Laguna still had traces of the Summer of Love.

Duff banged my car door on the high curb, "I'm so sorry."

Like a *Dukes of Hazzard* he hopped over the door. A car squealed to a stop, leaving a patch of acrid smelling rubber. Afraid to open my door into traffic, I too, vaulted over the door and onto the sidewalk. Another car screeched to a stop to get a look at us bare-chested beach boys. Duff was both proud and jealous that his new friend could also stop traffic.

Years later, after we had lived together for a while, "Stopping traffic," was a game we played to pass the boredom of the off season in a resort town. Like Midwestern kids dropping watermelons from a bridge into oncoming traffic, Duff and I would drop our boardshorts beside my car on Pacific Coast Highway. One day a Corvette rear-ended a Cadillac and I was struck by flying fiberglass. I still have the scar.

"Oh My God!" Duff screamed. "That's Tab Hunter."

Later that evening the two of us were dining at the movie star Tab Hunter's home overlooking Dana Point Harbor, just south of Laguna Beach.

But back to the day I met Duff Paddock. I suggested we measure the skid marks to see who had caused the longest.

Duff shook his head no, "I don't play that game. Whose is bigger."

I laughed, knowing already that I've won.

"I've got to pay Cory," Duff said urgently.

I followed Duff up the steps that lead behind the Bead Shop. In the cool shade from an old tree overhead, we squeezed between the bead shop and a wooden fence that hid the bungalow on the other side. My bare feet were tortured further by the hard little acorns that had fallen from the tree above us. The tears in my eyes blurred my view of Duff's perfect ass, only inches away.

Just like West Street Beach, Duff's home was a hidden paradise. A tiny, weathered bungalow sat on a rise in a forgotten neighborhood that must have once had a front yard that ran to the Coast Highway. At some point they built shops where the front lawn had been, surrounding these forgotten bungalows behind a fortress of storefronts.

"Hey Co!" Duff called into the open house.

We were standing on a termite rotted wooden porch. It creaked under our feet, as if it would give way at any minute. Water dripped from a jungle of plants hanging from macrame planters. No wonder the porch felt spongey.

"Hello Gorgeous," a tall, skinny girl dramatically threw her arms around Duff. Her hands are covered to the elbow in hot pink Playtex rubber gloves. She is wearing a black bikini and her periwinkle blue eyes are twinkling as she looks me over.

"Co is playing French Maid, today," Duff says by way of introduction.

"My name is Cori," She says extending her hand to me, struggling to pull off the rubber glove.

"I'm Dave Churchill," I say leaning in to kiss her cheek so that she doesn't have to fuss with her glove. She blushes as bright as her pink gloves.

Duff counts out four $20 bills to Cori.

"I'm not a maid." She says to me. "I just wanted the pair of Reeboks that are in the Hobie's window downtown," Cori explained, "I work at Deignet's," she says with a French accent.

"Co works at Denny's," Duff clarifies for me.

I can't believe my good fortune, I've made two new friends in one single day. I thought at this moment that I had made friends for life.

"I work at the Marina Pacifica Multiplex in Seal Beach." I add to the conversation. Soon I've agreed to treat my new friends to a showing of, *"The Other Side of Midnight."*

Things were happening fast.

Duff was giving me a tour of his bungalow. He had inherited the place from a lover who had moved back to San Francisco.

"Oh, Marc," Cori says dreamily.

"Marc Bowers," Duff says wistfully. "He took the car and I have to come up with his half of the rent."

I come to find out that his half of the rent is only $90. It turns out the back bedroom is rented to a nurse named Pat Downs who is never home.

"You could convert this unused dining room into a bedroom," Cori is saying, gesturing like Carol Merrill on *Let's Make a Deal*. "Do you have a car?"

She smiles conspiratorially at Duff when I say, "I have a convertible."

"Then it's all settled!" Cori proclaims.

"Duffy's driver's license was revoked when he met Marc in Sacramento."

Realizing I'm being tag-teamed, and not in the good way, I say, "But, I don't have a job, so I can't."

Even though gas is only 49 cents a gallon, I could not afford to drive back and forth 50 miles to Seal Beach on a movie usher's pay.

"I'll get you a job with me!" Duff says, "I valet park cars at the Hotel Laguna."

I make my getaway and jump in my open convertible and head up the Coast Highway as the sun sets in the Pacific.

In my rearview mirror, I see Cori's pink gloved hand waving goodbye like a Rose Queen.

"Buh Bye, Seal Beach Dave".

This Town | CHAPTER 4

Before that week ended I was a Lagunatic. I was no longer Seal Beach Dave. I had packed my record albums and my high school clothes and moved into Duff Paddock's dining room at 812 B South Coast Highway, Laguna Beach, CA 90254.

I was 19-years old. I managed a transfer from Golden West College to Saddleback College. The semester had just ended for the summer, it was not yet Memorial Day. This was the first time I had merged my record collection with another's. Linda Ronstadt was now between Grace Jones and Donna Summer. These were arranged in alphabetical order, starting with Joan Armatrading.

My bed was pressed against the wall in the corner of the open dining room. This left a path for my roommates to make midnight runs to the refrigerator. I rarely saw the 3rd Roommate, Pat Downs, he was a nurse and worked odd hours.

I would suspect the Joan Armatrading and Janis Ian were his. Once I moved in, I rarely saw Duff. His dance card was full.

I'd only see him at work. True to his promise, he got me a job working beside him as a valet parker at the Hotel Laguna, just off Main Beach. I don't recall interviewing for the job. I suspect the only qualification was to look foxy in tight white tennis shorts. Forty years later, I am certain of that.

Duff Paddock didn't possess a driver's license, and yet here we were parking cars.

It was a dream job. I never met a manager. We were unsupervised. We stood along Coast Highway and watched the expensive cars go by. And they watched us. We became as much of a fixture in Laguna as The Greeter, the old man who waved at cars as they entered town.

We always had cash in our pockets. Duff kept his in his front pocket to give the illusion of a basket. We were getting paid to stop traffic.

The Hotel Laguna was a faded grand hotel in the Moorish style on the ocean just south of Main Beach. As an indication it had seen better days, rarely did anyone arrive with a trunk full of luggage on an extended vacation. I never once saw a bellboy in all the years I worked there. I don't recall anyone ever checking in.

There were a few guests that would retreat with our foxy straight co-worker to the little booth where we kept the car keys. Their Jaguar would be idling in the drive. I didn't have a clue what they were doing (I was extremely naive. As I write this, now I can see they were buying blow or blow jobs).

Other guests would pay for the convenience to park near the many restaurants and boutiques in downtown Laguna. They would pretend to shop the dusty old boutiques that lined the hotel's arcade. This was a simple ruse as Ruth's Millinery was the only store still operating in 1979. Ruth's rose-colored '58

Fleetwood Sixty-Special was my favorite car to park. Let Duff and the other guy fight over the Lamborghini Ghiblis and Ferrari Daytonas. Ruth still tipped with change from her coin purse. She would snap it shut like a bank vault.

While Duff's pockets bulged with dollar bills like John Holmes, mine jingled like reindeer. I don't remember wanting for anything in that summer of 79.

Except, I wanted a boyfriend. It became clear to me that Duff would never be my boyfriend. Soon, I was spending nights home alone with Joan Armatrading and Janis Ian. At 19, I was already a bitter old queen.

I was so pathetic, that Duff took pity on me, "Do you want to come with me to Terry Causey's?" he'd reluctantly ask.

I'd shake my head no, resignedly like Susan Hayward in *I Want To Live.* I wasn't sure if Duff invited me because he needed a ride. Regardless, I did not want to sit around watching old people sniff cocaine. I pulled the covers up and sank into my melancholy. I hoped that Duff would be home in time to go to the beach in the morning.

We didn't have curtains, set back in the lost neighborhood we didn't need them for privacy. I woke to the screech of the turntable needle skipping at the end of the Joan Armatrading album. Blinded by the sun that flooded the house. Surrounded by trees and the macrame plant hangers, Duff's bedroom was pitch dark. I was on my way to the beach by the time Duff dragged himself home.

"Don't forget, we're working at the Royal Hawaiian restaurant tonight." Duff said as we passed.

Although I had never met a manager, Duff seemed to receive memos from the boss overnight, "Just wear your white shorts and an Aloha Shirt."

At the gay beach, I joined the sad migration of service industry workers leaving at mid-afternoon. I was forced to decline invitations to a dinner for Egon Von Furstenberg, extended to me in Duff's absence.

"Son of a bitch!" Duff moaned.

"I forgot to pick up the Aloha shirts."

Freshly showered, we had just rubbed Manoi oil on each other. This Tahitian coconut oil smelled like a Hawaiian Lei, a mix of Pikkake and Frangipani. Glistening like Island boys we ran a block down the street to buy some aloha shirts at Tippecanoe's Thrift Shop. We were running late for the restaurant's opening. While we impatiently waited at the stoplight beside Albertson's grocery, we were invited to cook-outs by men waving steaks from a brand-new Mercedes-Benz.

"Your meat is too tiny to get my attention," Duff quipped of the Porterhouse brandished from the car window.

We climbed the railroad ties laid into the hillside to get to Tippecanoes. This store was a rundown shack perched on a cliff that creaked and snapped as we hurriedly browsed through the dusty merchandise. Duff and I both grabbed for the same seafoam green Reyn-Spooner shirt printed with hibiscus. I let go in fear, when the building seemed to shift under our weight and threatened to slide down the cliff. I settled for an indigo blue one in the same pattern. I considered it a win that mine didn't smell as musty as Duff's.

Like Batman and Robin, Duff and I leapt into my convertible and raced north on Coast Highway to the Royal Hawaiian restaurant. As if we were the dynamic duo, onlookers stopped and gawked as the blonde and brunette sped through town with our hair billowing like superhero capes.

No sooner had we parked in the empty lot, than a line of cars started to pull in behind us. We quickly went to work to quiet the honking horns of the frustrated early birds. Desperately trying to clear the back up, I struggled with the stick shift of a Jensen Interceptor. It was blocking the entrance.

Pacific Coast Highway had come to a standstill, with cars attempting to turn into our parking lot. A police car pulled alongside and scolded us over its loudspeaker. His stern voice drowned out the sound of my grinding the clutch on the Jensen. I noticed Duff fixing his hair in the vanity mirror of a Mark V, while also powdering his nose. Within 20 minutes our pockets were bulging with car keys. Neither of us could remember which cars they belonged to. We already had about fifty cars. Mercedes keys were easy to recognize in the 1970's as they had a rubber end on the key. Cadillacs had a wreath and crest logo stamped into their keys. We panicked. We had no clue which key went with which car. With the ingenuity of Lucy and Ethel we decided to leave the keys in the car, so that we would know which ones matched.

Before we could start pairing keys to cars, a parade of diners started to leave after happy hour, while cars continued coming in. Lucky for us, most of the customers were sauced on Mai Tais and didn't seem to care that we had no clue what we were doing.

Since I was a car nut, I remembered that the florid bald man with the busty blonde drove the Dumbarton green Eldorado convertible. This was the first time I was tipped a $5 bill. A chubby Hawaiian boy in an Aloha shirt was wheeling a kiosk past the increasingly agitated queue of patrons.

"Duffy you must use this!" He was shouting in pidgin.

Duff abandoned his trek to retrieve someone's car, tossed the keys to me and reversed direction.

"I'm sorry, Junior," Duff apologized flirtatiously to the son of the restaurant's owner.

"Which car?" I shouted to Duff, waving the car keys he had just thrown me.

Duff just shrugged his shoulders. "It's the Continental, you moron." The customer yelled.

His date turned her back to him and chatted with another couple. Junior was wagging his finger at Duff. I gracefully pulled the Continental around. I didn't bother to wait for the driver to stiff me on the tip, I ran to the passenger side and opened the suicide doors for the lady and the other couple. They each gave me a wad of bills and apologized for the driver's attitude.

Duff beat me to the handsome blonde guy and quickly rushes over to me, "Did you see who that is?" Duff asks with a slack jaw, "That's the Marlboro Man."

I recognize him only as the man with the Jensen whose clutch I burned out. I was happy to leave him to Duff. As Duff pulled the Interceptor around I could still smell the burnt clutch. There was a brief lull once we got those customers sorted.

I suggested we try to match keys to the cars. Duff and I each started with a handful of keys. I tried mine in the door lock, but Duff got in each car and tried to start the ignition. Assuming my way was faster, I was going to suggest it to Duff when I realized he was doing key bumps in each car.

I panicked when a Mercedes 450 SL blew into the parking lot with *Bad Girls* by Donna Summer blaring. The blonde girl behind the wheel was singing along at the top of her lungs. She'd honk the horn in unison every time Donna Summer sang, "Toot Toot, Beep Beep."

"No Waaay!" Duff screams running towards the topless European car. "Co, where'd you get this?"

Cori says "Get in!" The first time I had met this girl she was wearing pink rubber gloves and cleaning Duff's house. Now she is driving us in a new Mercedes-Benz roadster. I had folded myself onto the package shelf behind the front seats. I was leaning forward between my new friends to hear what they were saying over the rush of wind and the crash of surf. The lights of Laguna were a blur behind me as we drove further away from our job. Cori told us that she got a new job as an Au Pair for some rich doctors with two little kids.

"Jordan and Samantha, they are so adorable."

"We better get back to work," I say panicked.

"I can get you a new job," Cori says.

Before my semester starts at Saddleback College, I do have a new job.

I am the general manager of the Shoals Oceanfront Inn.

This rundown efficiency motel on a bluff overlooking the beach is a tax write-off for the two doctors Cori now works for, Nadine and Jerry Levinson.

Because it is a tax write-off they pay me an unimaginable amount of money for two days work a week. Because I hesitated in accepting, they agreed to work around my college schedule. Because I was fearful of losing my tan, they agreed to put a phone line by the pool.

Duff was Beauty as Anarchy, he was a catalyst of chaos for making things happen. I would not have the life I had, had I not met Duff.

Soon, Duff met Dean and everything changed.

West Street Beach 1979 | CHAPTER 5

West Street Beach was my place in the sun. After miserable teenage years as a gay boy in a gray town, I had grown into a golden boy. I put on muscle, I had a deep dark Coppertone tan, and my hair bleached white blonde on the volleyball court. Unlike in the steel town where I grew up, "Volleyball is for girls," the football jocks sneered, Californians revered volleyball players as gods.

It was easy to believe that on West Street Beach. We were looked at with lust and envy—a poisonous combination unique to the gay man. The volleyball court on West Street beach was situated on the highest point of the beach (Thanks, Bo Frieden).

When you played you felt as if you were on Mount Olympus. The world's most beautiful men were literally at your feet, laying on the sand. In 1979 West Street Beach was covered with cover models and packed with porn stars. Standing 6'3" on this highest point, it felt like I was surveying my kingdom. It was just as magical as any in Greek Mythology. A crescent of sand nestled between two rock outcroppings, buttressed by high cliffs.

A cerulean ocean stretched to the horizon dotted with bobbing white sailing yachts. The "favorites" of the gods frolicked in the surf.

From the court I could hear the invitations to a hundred parties. Coquettish giggles echoed off the surrounding cliffs, drowned out by the crashing of the surf and the staccato beat of the volleyball. I witnessed love affairs begin and end. Unable to stop them I anticipated train wrecks coming.

Directly west at the tideline, like a spider, Stephen Henderson had woven his web. A dinosaur from another epoch, he recreated a St. Tropez beach club around his towel. He reclined on a pink-striped backrest—a souvenir purloined from the Royal Hawaiian Hotel on Waikiki. A massive boom box barricaded him like the Sheraton Waikiki. A Thermos of martini's was always at hand. Like the *House of the Rising Sun*, he'd been the ruin of many a poor boy.

Stephen was a tall Scandinavian with matinee idol looks gone to seed from a lifetime of debauchery. A word-of-mouth legend since the Broadway premier of Hair in 1968. A decade later fans were still gushing, "It is so big, you could see it from the last row of the balcony." Theater queens still said of his nude scene in the musical.

In his mid-thirties he surrounded himself with old friends and minor titles, lining up young men for Hollywood parties, "You must come, It's a party for Nuryev. Tonight, at Allan Carr's Hillhaven. He's only inviting 10's." The movie *10* was the current Julie Andrews release that made a star of Bo Derek.

Against my better judgement I found myself at the party between Mr. Teenage America and next year's Mr. Universe.

I dramatically crossed my legs and did my best Bo Frieden impression, "Darling, do you like my earrings?" Referring to the half-naked, oiled bodybuilders glistening on either side of me.

Bo Frieden was one of the old-timers on West Street Beach. He was my volleyball mentor. In his mid-fifties, he had the gym-built body and the presence of a winning football coach. He claimed to have fought in the 1948 Israeli War of Independence. He also claimed to have moved the volleyball courts to West Street Beach, singlehandedly creating this as the new gay beach. This he-man was often found bringing down the house at dinner parties, by demurely crossing his legs and holding handles of Smirnoff to his ears and asking, "Do you like my earrings?"

Unlike Stephen Henderson he nurtured poor boys in the ways of the gay world.

Bo was still a formidable player on the court. He'd gently bring my attention back to the game after it was lost tracking the newest arrival to the beach. A beautiful French boy with the coloring and ass of Duff Paddock, but with a heaving chest and pouting lips.

"Pay attention, Church." I was curious where he would choose to sit. He passed by the nubile twinks surrounding Cuban Marc and Jimmy Barton. Their towel amounted to a petting zoo, where the boys piled together on top of each other like puppies.

I had hoped Frenchie was a loner like me.

The Texan bodybuilders who set up camp in the same spot every weekend beckoned him over, he brushed them off. He was heading dangerously close to Stephen Henderson's web. This boy was a 10 if ever there was one.

"Church!" Bo called in the nick of time so that I received the serve that was coming straight at me.

We usually won the game, which meant we had to play again to face the challengers. After playing four hours straight in the hot sand, I'd need to take a quick dip in the ocean to cool off between games. This pissed off the challenging team who had been waiting hours to get on the court.

I would zig zag past that day's obsession on my way between towels to the water, today it was the French boy who had decided to sit alone.

"Church!" Scott Nelson would holler waving me back to the court.

I ignored him wanting to rinse off the sweat and sand, most importantly rinsing my hair in saltwater so that it got the perfectly bleached surfed-out blonde. As I slowly passed the French boy attempting to catch his eye. He arched his back to tease me.

My nemesis called out., "Quit cruising him Church. He's mine."

I raised my arm to shoot Scott Nelson the bird. A clump of sand fell off my arm and plopped on the boy's towel. He began frantically brushing my sand off his towel with a moue of distaste on his pillowy lips. This fussy reaction immediately disqualified him from my affections. I moved on towards the ocean.

I heard an unfamiliar Irish brogue ask "Why do they call him Church?"

"Doll," I heard George Smith's mellifluous baritone reply, "he's got more worshippers on their knees than Reverend Schuler at the Crystal Cathedral."

I was certain George, the only black man on the beach in the 1970's had pitched his reply so that I could hear as I walked past. George unabashedly flirted with me. He was always surrounded by ballet dancers. One of them, Anthony, was a fierce competitor on the volleyball court.

I elbowed my way past the squealing gym bunnies at the water's edge. "Ooh, it's so cold," they squealed, scooting away like so many silly sandpipers.

I dove under a wave. Dripping wet I made my way back to the volleyball court. I spotted a new object of lust and took a detour to check him out. This blonde, tanned beauty was wearing the just released Maui & Sons plaid volley shorts. With those cool trunks I was hopeful that a little sand wouldn't bother him.

Before I could wind my way to this new arrival another nemesis of mine had stopped to hit on him. Ray Harrington had planted his skim board in the sand next to the beauty like a conquering flag. From my perch on the volleyball court, I had watched Harrington drag his prop from towel to towel. I'd never once seen him actually ride it. Thwarted I ignored the new kid and beelined for the court.

"Hey Church," Ray Harrington called out.

I was certain he only acknowledged me so I would notice he had trapped the new beauty. "How's it, Harrington?" I responded, shaking my wet hair like a dog, splattering them both.

Ray's conquest whimpered at the spray of cold water. Ray Harrington glared at me like the Wicked Witch of the West. He might as well have shrieked "I'm Melting."

From the court Scott Nelson spotted what I had done. "Church, you're a bitch, but that was beautiful!"

We volleyball players were tyrants. In 1979, straight-acting men were in demand. Which is why we wore boardshorts instead of speedos. Why Ray Harrington dragged his skim board along the beach. Unlike, Ray we weren't an act. We played volleyball 8-10 hours a day, until the sun went down. We were too tired to hit the parties or pick up tricks at the Boom Boom Room.

But West Street Beach was its own party. Every day it was a festival like Coachella or Burning Man.

In the 1970's and early 1980's we put the Gay in Gay.

For an example, it seemed that nobody worked in the late 1970's. The beach was packed any day of the week. There was a group of regulars in their usual spots day after day. Larry was a schoolteacher, he reminded me of an ant, a round body with tiny arms and legs. He was deeply tanned and had a tiny head. Magpie was an advertising copywriter, he was friends with a man they called Flo. I had heard Flo was a GI in the Vietnam war. Through rain or shine they were in their same spot. From the volleyball court I'd watch theses spinster sisters plot and plan. Beginning in late fall they would be deep in whispered negotiations. Everything had to be top secret. For the last ten years they put on a pageant to officially open the beach on Memorial Day.

Even my friends who weren't beach goers came for this special day. Donnie McPhedran and Stevie B would join Duff Paddock and I. Donnie and Stevie B had day jobs. Neither of them cared for the sun. Donnie grew up in the desert of Arizona. Stevie B was mixed race who preferred his skin to be creamy white.

Under cover of darkness, Larry, Flo and Magpie strung a huge red ribbon between two palm trees, tied with a bow.

With great pomp and circumstance, this was to be cut with a giant pair of scissors at noon on Memorial Day to officially signal that the beach was open for the season.

Being a teenage brat, I found this absurd. Me and my friends along with hundreds of other gay boys had already stretched the ribbon aloft to get under it and onto the beach. In fact, I was already playing volleyball.

Bo Frieden palmed the volleyball in mid play, stopping the game, when he heard the trumpet fanfare. At the top of the hill, on the emergency road stood Larry and Flo. Larry was dressed in white tie and tails, he looked like the banker from Monopoly if the banker were a turtle. Flo was done up like Esther Williams in a fuchsia bathing suit and a large floppy brimmed hat. The entire beach was on their feet applauding wildly.

Hand in hand they tentatively made their way down the hill, it was obvious that Flo was having trouble navigating in high heels while lifting the brim of her hat to see where she was going.

The trumpeter continued his blowing. After fifteen minutes they were only halfway down the hill. A crowd of arriving beach goers were bottlenecked behind the procession. They threatened to push past, but Flo brandished her scissors at them. I attempted to wrest the volleyball from Bo's hands and continue the game, I was bored and bratty. Bo didn't need scissors to get me to back off.

Bo was standing ramrod straight with all the solemnity of a Marine at the tomb of the unknown soldier. I recognized this meant something important to him.

Today, I understand that after decades of repression, that procession acknowledged the first crumb of freedom. Before Stonewall it was illegal to "masquerade as a woman." It had also been illegal for two men to hold hands. Bo was acknowledging the strides that had been made. Larry was holding hands with a man dressed as a woman.

Like two hooligans in church, Duff and I tried to show respect. Like parishioners the rest of the beach sat back down. By 12:30 Larry and Flo had finally arrived at the ribbon. The trumpeter handed a megaphone to Larry. I wondered if he was a student of Larry's.

Over the megaphone Larry introduced himself as the Mayor of West Street Beach. "For the past decade it has been my pleasure to welcome all comers to West Street Beach."

Duff covers my mouth for laughing lewdly. Bo shoots me a stern look.

After a beat the rest of the beach erupts at the word comers.

"Today, our First Lady of Laguna, Flo," Larry pauses for applause.

Flo grabs for the megaphone. Larry continues, "Flo will cut the red ribbon to officially welcome all to the summer of 1979." Flo teeters on high heels in the sand.

Someone has sent giggling twinks around to distribute blotter acid from wicker baskets like incorrigible flower girls at a wedding. I watched the trumpeter take his.

By the time the ribbon was officially cut, the entire beach was tripping. The trumpeter took off his band uniform and jumped into the puppy pile by Cuban Marc and Jimmy Barton.

A deafening roar of motorcycle engines echoed off the cliffs surrounding the beach and brought the hallucinating crowd to its feet, preparing to run for their lives. West Street Beach had always been a safe sanctuary, away from gay bashing, despite the rising anti-gay sentiment then spreading in conservative Orange County thanks to the Briggs Initiative and Anita Bryant.

Instead of the Hell's Angels descending upon us, it was only a flotilla of drag queens on jet skis storming the beach from around the rock at Camel Point. Younger gays led by a curly haired blonde named Gregg decided to usurp the boring pageantry of the old guard. Their gold lame sarongs were whipping like flags behind them as they wove through the yachts bobbing offshore. With a thunderclap, a crashing wave flung them halfway up the beach.

Young gays were popping up from towels, like half-naked jack-in -the-boxes to avoid being run down by a beached jet ski. Someone's long blonde hair was crushed under one jet ski, a sobbing sister was desperately rounding up muscle men to help lift the jet ski off her missing sister. To everyone's relief, there was no body but only a blonde wig, which they began tossing around like a football.

A dazed drag queen screams, "That's mine!" She rushes into the group of musclemen. Like a linebacker in gold lame she tackles the one catching her wig. The crowd roars. Holding their wigs like Pom Poms, the drag queens do a cheer. High as kites the entire beach starts dancing to unheard music.

Because of the towering hills that surrounded the city, Laguna Beach was known as, "Radio Free Laguna," since no AM or FM signal could get past those hills. The only music heard was the crashing of the waves and the laughter of a thousand queens rising and falling like Callas. The volleyball and paddleball were all that kept the beat.

That is until Magpie brought a ham radio to the beach and began broadcasting as KWER FM. He played the latest new wave hits such as *Teenage Enema Nurse* on Queer FM. Soon, the entire beach was a mosh pit. One day, Magpie brought the infamous KROQ DJ Dusty Street to West Street and she broadcast live.

The tween trumpeter became the Falcon star Matt Gunther.

Just so you know, I did not drop acid that day. None of this was a hallucination. It really happened!

Michael Rotella | CHAPTER 6

Michael Rotella didn't require a jet ski to signal his arrival. He was a sensation the moment he stepped on the gay beach in Laguna in 1980. Like a tennis match audience, every head turned in unison. He appeared a golden-brown teddy bear of a young man in an old speedo and a cowboy hat.

"Dahling," stammered Steven Henderson in his best Tallulah Bankhead, "I can introduce you." I studiously avoided Steven Henderson in those days. Like *The House of the Rising Sun*, Steven had been the ruin of many a poor boy.

"Lady Ashtray is hosting a sunset soiree at the Surf & Sand to introduce Michael. And you can be my guest," Bob Ressitauer was known as Lady Ashtray to his intimates, "because he's had so many butts in his face."

Her suite at the Surf & Sand was packed like a clearance rack, with all of last season's Trophy Twinks. All eyes were on Michael Rotella as he warmed himself with the last of the sun's rays on the balcony. He was still in his threadbare speedo and cowboy hat. Everyone else was dressed to the nines in the latest brightly-colored Ralph Lauren Polo shirts.

All Michael needed to command attention was the exquisite pattern of his chest hair. There is a photo of him captured in the golden light of that summer day, I can still see it in my mind's eye. Like a movie star he knew how to command attention. I watched him commandeer the most flattering light. I'd never seen anyone with his presence.

I soon learned the secret of his Speedo, what made his more enticing than any of the other boy's on the beach. Michael took the concept of distressing our Levi's 501s and applied it to the Speedo. He ripped out the modesty panel lining and subjected the nylon to repeated washing and drying. All the elasticity of the fabric was ruined so that it just draped over his spectacular ass like an Hermes scarf.

That summer of 1980, there was a shortage of quarters in Laguna Beach as all the lesser beauties jammed the laundromats trying to ruin their brand-new Speedos to achieve the same effect. Michael was a trend-setter.

Chatting alone with Michael, I was so hypnotized by the swirling pattern of his chest hair. I found myself agreeing to whatever he suggested.

"Would you give me a ride home, tomorrow morning?"

Having been, before his arrival, one of the hunky numbers in town, I naturally assumed this was an invitation to spend the night.

"I'll be waiting for you at the valet at 10:00 AM," he clarified.

I was learning the prerogative of a star.

When I drove to the Surf &Sand to pick Michael Rotella up at 10:00 AM, he was still wearing the threadbare speedo and cowboy hat. His only luggage was a dozen overflowing shopping bags from the local luxury boutiques. He loaded these in the tiny trunk of my Camaro convertible. With a devilish grin, he leaped over the door of my convertible and into the backseat. As usual I misread this as an invitation. With his cowboy hat in his hand he made a forward motion which I understood as "Home James."

"Where am I taking you?" I had no idea where his home was or how far I would be driving him.

"Old Malibu Road."

It was impossible to make small talk in an open convertible with Donna Summer blaring.

"Here, play this!" Michael commanded. He handed me a cassette of *Alive on Arrival* by Steve Forbert. I was surprised this man-about-town wanted me to play an unknown singer/songwriter's folk album. That was Michael. He always defied expectations.

As we drove out Laguna Canyon Road, past the makeshift crosses planted on the side of the road to mark a tragic loss, I tried to parse the significance of two of the album's tracks, *"Tonight, I feel so far away from home."* And *"You cannot win if you do not play."* What was Michael attempting to reveal about himself?

Once we got on the 405 Freeway, the San Diego Freeway, heading north, Michael revealed his reason for taking the backseat.

He folded the seatback of the front passenger's bucket seat forward so that it rested on the dash. (Back in the day, this was the only way to get out of the backseat of a 2 door car.) But, Michael wasn't planning on exiting my speeding car. With a beach towel, he turned the folded front seat into a chaise lounge. He leaned against it, facing backwards into the sun. He threw his golden brown legs over the top of the rear seat and caught some rays. He treated the fifty minute drive to Malibu as if he were lounging on a yacht.

Perfecting a tan was a fulltime occupation for us 80's boys. Which is why we worked as little as possible.

"Make a left past Pepperdine and follow Old Malibu Road until you come to a beach house with an Oscar weathervane on the roof." Was all that Michael Rotella said to me.

After an hour in the car with Michael Rotella I was aching with desire. His every movement was sensual, like a drowsy cat.

"You can drop me off, here," When these words came out of his plush, pillowy lips I was crushed. I realized he was not going to invite me into this beachfront mansion.

On the lonely drive home, I had imagined Michael was a kept boy. I was a naïve nineteen. Michael was a worldly 26. I see now, that Michael may have intuitively tried to protect me.

The owner of the mansion with the Oscar weathervane turned out to be the producer of the movie *Grease*, the Fabulous Allan Carr.

Months later, I was invited inside. I attended a thirty-fifth birthday dinner given for the sinister Steven Henderson. After the caviar and Cristal, a cake and quaaludes were presented. Being a prude, I was asked to leave. A chauffeur drove me home before the presents were opened, which I assume were the three young friends I came with.

Like the big kid in the neighborhood, I think Michael tried to avoid introducing me to trouble. I would say Michael was street smart. I think he came from the outer boroughs of New York City. Although the 1970's were the "Me Decade," we didn't talk much about ourselves. The rumors that preceded Michael everywhere he went, seemed to suggest he had a glamorous Manhattan past.

Like a tough New Yorker, he knew all the wise guys in Hollywood. Instead of followers, Michael had hundreds of friends. He was close to the fedora-wearing fixer, attorney Harry Weiss, as well as Jeff Cole, the porn star Buster. That summer I found myself one of the moons orbiting Michael Rotella. Michael had a powerful gravity that pulled people to him. By virtue of knowing him you were on the A-List. Michael always knew the best parties. Like that day in Laguna he knew the correct time to make an entrance.

I never knew what Michael did for a living. All I know is that he made things happen. For years I carried his business card, translucent red plastic imprinted with *Spur of the Moment Catering* and a 213 area code. Along with Harry Weiss, Reb Brown and Ward Sylvester, Michael was involved with creating the first

Circuit Party, The Mothership Arrives held at Griffith Park, starring the Ritchie Family.

Going to parties was what we lived for in our early twenties. That, and going to the beach (which was a party). I was the only one in our circle going to college. Which is why I refer to Michael Rotella as a friend—he fits the Merriam-Webster definition.

The connotation of friend today, which implies a closeness, makes me feel presumptuous using it in regards to Michael Rotella. I wasn't around when he was sick or when he died.

Through today's lens, we would seem more like members of a flashmob. We'd assemble suddenly at a party or event, captivate the crowd and then quickly disperse. Our only choreography was the passing of a coke vial.

Which brings me to an example of Michael's kindness. I had mixed too many drugs and was having a bad trip. Michael left the party and took me to his apartment and talked me down for over an hour. He put on the Steve Forbert cassette. His apartment was a hi tech Taj Mahal. Hi Tech was a design style pioneered by the decorator Jay Steffe. It mixed an assortment of industrial finishes, like diamond plate linoleum against commercial grade carpet that one would find lining the walls of a freight elevator. Michael's apartment was done in fifty shades of gray. The centerpiece of Michael's apartment was a pedestal bed. It was as tall as an altar. I could only imagine the virgin sacrifices. (Remember I was coming down off a bad trip.) But, alas, I was not a virgin.

Which was irrelevant, because by this time Michael had taken a lover. He fell for a cornfed midwestern boy with cornsilk blonde hair, Michael Neff. The Michaels were the "Brangelina" of their day.

Michael Rotella seemed to settle happily into domestic life. At this time in the mid 1980's, he opened a restaurant on Santa Monica Blvd, in what used to be Boystown, but was now the brand-new City of West Hollywood. It was called Greenwich Village Pizzeria. It was between All American Boy and the new nightclub Rage.

The last time I saw Michael Rotella was at a party at Duff Paddock's on Sunset Plaza. He had introduced a protégé of attorney Harry Weiss to an ex-girlfriend of mine. They subsequently married.

In a fit of pique, I dropped Michael. Ridiculous I know, since I am and always have been gay. I lost touch with Michael and only heard a rumor that he had died of AIDS.

Get Your Kicks On Route 66 | CHAPTER 7

Unsure of myself, and yet, always certain I was right. I was a difficult friend and an impossible roommate. By now, we all lived together in Donnie's three-bedroom condo in Dana Point. Duff, Dean, Stevie B and me. I no longer slept in a dining room, I now slept in a breakfast nook. There was a fifth roommate, Rick, who kept to himself (either by choice or by fiat).

After the Go-Go's incident at Emerald Bay, we were too hungover and ashamed to show our faces on West Street Beach. For the first time we missed the annual opening of the beach on Memorial Day. Our shared landline rang all day long. We slept through it. Our answering machine had 23 new messages.

BEEP.

"Girl! you missed it!"

BEEP.

"Michael Rotella was a no show. Harry Weiss took him to Palm Springs."

BEEP.

"Poor Flo was sick as a dog, but she still showed up in wig and heels to cut the ribbon. What's your excuse, bitch?"

BEEP.

"Duff. Call me immediately."

BEEP.

"Bubbie, it's Bo. Are you OK? It's not like you to miss a volleyball day. Hopefully you are shacked up with a humpy number."

BEEP.

"This Message is for David Churchill. It's Larry Lane calling from Cocoa Beach. Michael Tholl is jetting us out to surprise Bo Frieden on his birthday. Call me back. We want to make reservations at your motel. Thanks."

BEEP.

"Duff. It's important call me."

BEEP.

"Dave. I'm surfing T Street in San Clemente and I'm horny. Do you wanna do it? It's Hal Story."

BEEP.

"Dahlink, it's moi, Stephen. Burt Hixon is down from Redondo. He's taking his yacht out for a sunset cruise in Dana Point Harbor. There will be an 8-ball. I've got a jar of Ludes. Bring only 10's. And Camille. We cast off at 6:00 sharp."

BEEP.

"Steve, it's me Jim. I'm not mad anymore. Come back. It's not your fault. Calvin found his vial. I'll make it up to you. Whatever you want."

BEEP.

"Duff. Call me. They busted Terry for coke."

BEEP.

"Girlfriend, it's R.D. Those travel agents I told you about from Long Island have a brick of cocaine. They want me to bring some boys. We're in Treasure Island. I know, it's tacky. Their trailer is a double wide. Hurry up! they are drawing lines of coke the length of your dick. Just pull it out and lay in on the mirror. Tragic Kurt has his out now. It's a dick of death. He insists they make the line as thick as his dick. Hurry. I've left your name at the gate. #29"

I insisted that our partying was getting out of hand. Laguna was going to be the death of us.

"Road Trip!" I suggested.

"Miami!" Duff seconded.

His lover Dean Frey harrumphed.

"And New Orleans!" Donnie chimed in.

Stevie B said, "I'll get Jim's Mercedes 280 SE sedan. He said anything I want."

Jim Moniz always lent Stevie B his 450SL roadster, we'd tool around Laguna with the Go-Gos blasting *"This town is our town, it is so glamorous, bet you'd live here if you could and be one of us!"*

Donnie's trick of the night politely asked, "May I come along?" Hopeful that this romance was the real thing, Donnie happily agreed.

John from Santa Barbara brought our number to six. There was no room for my date from that night. I was painfully aware that Rob Kreuger had no desire to be promoted from trick to boyfriend. He had already driven back to Hollywood that morning. I would be the only one alone.

We were agreed. Giddy with anticipation, I got out a map and began planning our route. Gas was only .98 cents, and motels were under $20. Duff and the boys meticulously packed their outfits. I calculated we ought to be able to do it for $250 each. I had friends in Cocoa Beach Florida who I was certain would put us up. Between the six of us we had never lacked an invitation to spend the night before. I didn't calculate that I was the only one of us still single.

Jim Moniz wasn't persuaded to loan us his luxury sedan. "But, he's reserved a suite for us at the New Orlean's Hilton."

Stevie B tried to save face, "And, he'll treat us to dinner at Galatoire's."

"That's OK," I said, "his Mercedes only seats five. It has that damn console."

Without thinking, I suggested we take my 12-year-old Camaro convertible, "There is no console between the bucket seats, six of us will fit if someone sits on the hump."

"Don't look at me!" Donnie screamed.

"We'll draw straws," I said, certain that I would be in the driver's seat. "It *is* my car!" I was prepared to protest.

My 1969 Camaro was washed and waxed and looked brand-new. It was a beautiful dark Verduro Green. I hadn't bothered to check under the hood. A metaphor for my life in those days. The luggage my five friends meticulously packed wouldn't fit in the tiny trunk. Claws were out when I suggested we remove 7 items a piece to help make it fit. Defiantly, Donnie removed the spare tire, instead. Now everything fit. Satisfied, Donnie slammed the trunk lid. The trunk shut, but the hinge broke loose at the window.

"For Chrissakes," I screamed. "Get rid of some clothes!"

Since most of us wore mediums, we agreed to consolidate our Ralph Lauren polo shirts. The biggest argument occurred over Solids vs. Stripes. Do we stick with just this season's new solid colors or mix in some striped ones. Despite the battle for Ralph Lauren, we didn't wear shirts when we squeezed into the car to leave. My convertible did not have air conditioning. I ceded control of the tape player to Donnie, since it was between his legs on the hump. He relished this victory. The victory was mine, because the casette tapes were.

Tucson, Arizona was to be our first stop. Donnie had arranged for us to stay with some of his friends from Bisbee. I was happy I brought my cowboy hat.

My Camaro suffered under the weight of six boys, it's once powerful 350 V8 struggled to break the double nickel speed limit.

It bottomed out as it crossed the expansion gaps of the freeway. Donnie groaned as the transmission hump pounded his ass.

"You've been pounded harder than that!" I quipped, immediately regretting it. Donnie elbowed me in the ribs nodding towards his new boyfriend. It was bad form to reference a friend's past when he's trying to land a new boyfriend. Without a seat to sit on, Donnie's back was supported by Dean's knees from the backseat.

"It's too hot!" Dean whined. My convertible didn't have air conditioning. We were somewhere between Barstow and Needles. We were in the Mojave Desert at high noon in the summer. Temps were in the triple digits. We were blonde. We hadn't considered this.

But, we weren't totally stupid.

We pulled off Route 66 to put the convertible top up. The shade helped. In 1981, Route 66 still featured water stations spaced along the open road. Here you could get well water to fill your overheated radiator. Duff and Dean soaked a towel and wore it over their head to keep cool. They looked like sexy Arabs.

By the time we got to Phoenix, we had missed Donnie's friends in Tucson. From a payphone, there was no answer at their house. Donnie thought he remembered where they lived.

"It's a pink house with a cactus in front." After circling the same block for the third time, Donnie was forced to admit, "Maybe they painted it."

"For Fuck's Sake, Donnie, every house has a cactus!" Duff bellyached.

We decided to look for them at a gay bar. We had bought a Damron Guide—a popular directory of gay bars and cruisy areas throughout North America.

We found a gay bar on Speedway. We found Speedway using a map from Triple A. We didn't find Donnie's friends.

"You tired tramp!" Donnie screamed at me. "We could have had a bed to sleep in, if you didn't suddenly take a vow of chastity."

I had declined an invitation to spend the night with a snaggle-toothed rodeo clown. (Laguna Beach had spoiled me with its abundance of cover boys and physique models). Drunk and miserable my friends piled back into my little car once again.

Under the dim light of the bar's back door, Duff and Dean were having one of their famous lover's quarrels. The boys in the backseat were all passed out drunk and snoring. Dean was threatening Duff with a tumbleweed. I started the car and revved the engine to break it up. Dean threw the tumbleweed at Duff's feet. The loud noise it made startled me. Like a lightbulb exploding when dropped. It broke into a million pieces like a dandelion in the wind. Dean got into the passenger seat and locked the door on Duff. I let Duff in on my side, after all he was my friend. We drove out of the parking lot, just before a police cruiser arrived. I was relieved we didn't pass out drunk in the car to spend the night.

"Where are we going?" Dean turned his frustration on me.

Honestly, I had no idea. "I'm gonna keep driving towards the Grand Canyon."

I loved driving in the middle of the night. The roads were empty with only the occasional big rig. In the darkness it was nice and cool. It would have been quiet too, if Duff and Dean would only quit bickering.

"I don't need to see the Grand Canyon. I live with one!" Dean spit.

Jealousy was the drug that fueled their relationship. Duff led Dean to believe that he took on the most well-endowed men.

"It was as big as a Rutabega," I once heard him say to get under Dean's skin. This definitely got under mine. I still can't shop a produce aisle without thinking of what I missed.

I suddenly realized nobody was pressed against me perspiring. "Oh Shit! , Did we leave Donnie?"

I did a U-turn and headed back to the bar. This sudden maneuver woke everybody up.

"I'm back here!" Donnie had secreted himself into the hollow behind the backseat where the convertible top folds into.

"It's like sleeping in a hammock back here." This was the only time I wished that I were not 6'3".

Take It On The Run | CHAPTER 8

We made it halfway to the Grand Canyon. It was the middle of the night. I fought to stay awake while each of my friends snored. We got safely to a rest area. I lay my head against the window expecting to fall fast asleep. A shadow of a man passed by my window, groping his root vegetable. Now, I was wide awake. There were dozens of men loitering around the rest area. I knew what was going on. I wasn't as naïve as I pretended.

If I had consulted our Damron Guide, I would have known that this rest stop would be listed as a 'Cruisy' area. Before Grndr men came looking for a sex partner at public rest areas. I decided to forage for root vegetables. Maybe I would find a boyfriend here.

I slipped out of the car so as not to wake my friends. I wanted them to think I was saving myself for true love.

Like a wolf on the hunt, my senses were alert. My nerve endings tingled. The night was cooler but the desert air remained sensuously warm. I was still wearing the Quiksilver boardshorts that I had left Laguna in. That was all I had on. The warm wind ruffled the hair that was beginning to grow on my chest. The rest area was pitch dark at 4:00AM. I had never seen so many stars in the sky. I thought I'd seen fireflies, but it was just the glow of men smoking cigarettes.

I wandered between picnic benches where men were sitting with legs spread. I was careful not to make eye contact. My eyes were cast to the ground looking out for rattlesnakes. The danger thrilled me. Just out of my teens, I was used to being the hunted instead of the hunter. Bare-chested, I leaned against a mesquite tree with one leg up. This was a practiced pose that brought men to their knees. If only I smoked. A burning cigarette made the pose more menacing. The lighted tip was a beacon in the shadows. It made it easier for the men to find you. Sometimes this went horribly wrong. Too many of the Marlboro Men trying to look macho went all Bette Davis with their cigarettes. Instead of appearing butch, they looked like they were waving sparklers.

Tonight, the men were wearing Western shirts or wife-beaters. They didn't need a cigarette to look macho. Their tight Wranglers emphasized their baskets. Unlike my friends, I didn't look at the crotch first, I searched their eyes. I was still looking for love. I couldn't see their eyes in the shadows cast by their cowboy hats. I was impossible to tell if they were cute in the dark of night.

They appeared to be grown men, twice my age. This could be dangerous. The men came out from the shadows and circled around me in ever tightening circles. The confident ones reached out to cop a feel. It felt good to be desired. I was still safely outside the adobe restroom—I could run if I had to.

"Looky here! We got ourselves a chicken," a heavy-set trucker said in a deep smoker's voice as he pinned me against the tree. "Is that a gun in your pocket or are you just happy to see me?" he vamped like Mae West.

He dropped to his knees, grimacing as his joints cracked. He struggled to find a zipper to undo. I chuckled, this desert dweller had never encountered a Velcro fly before. I didn't want to go through with the deed. I just wanted him to want me. The Velcro fly on my boardshorts didn't save me. He just yanked my trunks down around my ankles. The other men gathered around to watch. This excited me. I got even harder when they formed a queue.

"Next," I called, cockily pushing his head away.

"Uh Oh!" The snaggle-toothed rodeo clown pushed his way from the end of the line. I pulled my trunks up and ran back to the car.

"Hey Jailbait, get your candy ass back here!" I recognized the rage of rejection and started to run faster. I ran right into Duff. With his alabaster skin, he looked obscenely naked. With my tan, I looked like I could be wearing a brown shirt. Duff's nipples and belly button were lewdly visible in the moonlight.

"Don't," I implored him.

Duff sashayed towards the group of men like a cheerleader walking into the player's locker room on a Friday night. Debbie from Denton couldn't wiggle her ass like Duff did. "D'ya want some fries with that shake?" the men catcalled.

With Duff and Donnie out of the way I sprawled across both front seats and slept dreamlessly. At dawn I woke up to the sound of a loon on a lake. Because we were in the desert there wouldn't be a lake, and this couldn't be a loon. It was only Dean honking out "Hon?" A familiar call that I recognize when Dean was trying to locate his honey, Duff. I had heard this call in strange bedrooms after a house party. I'd even recognized it soaring over a disco beat at a bathhouse. Soon I would hear it echo down the haunted streets of New Orleans. "Hon, where have you been?"

"Jeez, I just got up to use the restroom," Duff's fib was revealed once we got to the Grand Canyon.

My friend couldn't stop himself from needling me about what I missed by passing up the snaggletooth Rodeo Clown. "It was bigger than a rutabaga!" Duff taunted me.

"What is?" Dean demanded.

"Yes, Dean that *is* the $64,000 question, what is bigger than a rutabaga?"

Duff struggled to conceal his lie.

"An Eggplant!" Duff answered his own agricultural question. I always forgot he grew up with growers in the Sacramento Valley.

Today, I wonder if the Eggplant Emoji, could be Duff's legacy.

Dean Frey | CHAPTER 9

Dean Frey was dreamy. He was tall, dark and handsome. He came out of the exclusive Pacific Palisades of Los Angeles where Ronald Reagan was a neighbor. He was quiet and straight-acting (all-important qualities in that era.) He was a good volleyball player -the Palisades was home to Will Roger's State Beach, a volleyball mecca.

There was a gay beach at Will Roger's, nicknamed Ginger Roger's, but Dean somehow found his way to West Street Beach in Laguna. And Duff found him.

"But, he straightens his hair," I jabbed. I was young and ignorant. I was jealous.

Duff and Dean declared themselves Lovers, then they moved away together. Duff was the first friend I lost to a lover. I was inconsolable and unprepared to live without him in my daily life. Little did I know that Duff was preparing me for a future of losing friends.

Duff and Dean set up house in a 1920's courtyard apartment in Belmont Shores behind Ripples. They both took jobs at the popular oceanfront gay bar. We used to derisively call it Wrinkles, because the clientele was much older than we were. Not only did this bar pay the rent, it fueled the drama their relationship thrived on. I rarely saw them during this honeymoon as they were often quarrelling.

On the beach we would hear the latest gossip about DuffandDean (all one word).

The gay bar circuit was small back then. Thursday nights were Rumer Hazzit in Garden Grove, Saturday nights were Studio One in West Hollywood. Our crowd only went to Ripples if they didn't have enough gasoline to get to Studio One. 1979 was the year of gas rationing in California, one could only get gas on even or odd numbered dates, depending on the last number of your license plate. This led to some funny catastrophes, Cori was allowed to drive our boss's 450 SL Mercedes-Benz roadster. It only had a half a tank so we could only make it to Ripples in Long Beach. While we danced to Cheryl Lynn's *Star Love*, I watched Duff and Dean shimmy through the crowd with a tray full of drinks.

When the bar closed, they were screaming at each other, "You made more tips because you took off your shirt!"

They carried their lover's quarrel into the parking lot to our Mercedes. Most of the bar came to watch. At 20, I thought the world revolved around us, but they just came out to get in their own cars. Cori realized we only had enough gas in the Mercedes to get us back to Laguna.

"Nadine will kill us if we bring it home empty!" she panicked. It was the middle of the night on the wrong numbered day of the week.

"Start sucking," Cori handed me the rubber siphon hose that was the year's De Rigueur accessory as much as a Paloma Picasso necklace. I found myself once again cruising this notorious parking lot looking for something to suck. Soon, I was on my knees sucking gas out of a Chevy Chevette. It was difficult to prime without getting a mouthful of Ethyl.

"If that's the best you can do, I get why you don't have a boyfriend," Duff said.

"I'm a pitcher, not a catcher," I defended myself.

The next time I saw Duff and Dean, I heard the familiar honk of the loon in the quad at Cal State Long Beach, "Hon, wait up!"

"I didn't know you went to college." I knew little about the boy I considered my best friend, turns out he had completed an AA degree in Sacramento, and had enough credits to transfer to Cal State University, Long Beach. I thought I was the only one in our crowd that was college material.

"We got student loans!" Dean bragged. Now, it all made sense. I had my friends back!

On that quad my friends openly held hands in 1979. Like gay three musketeers we strode the campus in OP shorts and Polo shirts. When the student loan money evaporated, Duff and Dean moved in with Donnie and us in Dana Point. I was the only one to graduate. Dean was not the brightest bulb, which you will soon see when we get to Fort Lauderdale.

Is That All There Is? | CHAPTER 10

As it turned out that rest stop was near a ghost town called Beaver Creek. "Beaver Creek, my ass!" Duff laughed. "More like Boner Creek!"

Dean ignored this, but Donnie's ears perked up. Even though Donnie had brought along a potential new boyfriend, the siren of a strange dick was still strong. Certain he had missed out last night, Donnie wanted to stop at every rest stop. We couldn't drive past a rest area without Donnie insisting he needed to go potty.

John demanded we pull over at a K-Mart to buy some Imodium, "I don't have diarrhea!" Donnie protested, "I just have a small bladder."

"We'll get some Stop-Leak instead at a service station."

As young gay boys we didn't have role models, the elders on the beach encouraged sexual liberation. Bo Frieden was always pointing out the hottest number on the beach, suggesting that was what I go after. Monogamy was for straight people. Gay marriage was not even a remote possibility in 1981. What was valued was landing a boyfriend with the biggest root vegetable. "He has a dick of death," was the ultimate accolade. Some aspired to be a famous pair of lovers like Duff and Dean, the homosexual ideal. All I wanted was to find my soulmate.

We never talked about our dreams. I couldn't tell you if I even had one. I was majoring in Journalism—I thought I wanted to be a writer. I had no clue what Duff and Dean were majoring in. I suspected they were only in college to secure a student loan to pay for their own apartment. They both embraced the lavish lifestyle of the Dynasty Decade.

Despite Donnie's bladder we eventually made it to the Grand Canyon.

Gazing at this natural wonder, I finally understood Peggy Lee's *Is That All There Is?*

Stevie B, immersed in the Damron Guide, was agitating to get to Dallas, "Their Gay bar is called JR's. Sue Ellen's is for lesbians." Steve wanted fun before we had to rendezvous with his sugar daddy in two days in New Orleans, "Enough of these big holes," they complained, "let's meet some guys."

"Ha!" I spit, "you're only gonna find more big holes in Dallas."

The Texans I had met on the beach were notorious catchers. Catchers are what we called bottoms back in our day.

I took the long way to Dallas, I drove through the Texas panhandle. I wanted to see the famous roadside art installation in Amarillo called Cadillac Ranch.

Something I did learn in college. A collective of artists called Ant Farm buried 10 Cadillacs, nose down in the Texas dirt on a ranch visible from Interstate 10. The cars ranged from 1949 to 1963 and traced the evolution of the Cadillac tail fin.

"C'mon, it's out of our way!"

My friends didn't share my obsession with automobiles. To my surprise they realized I had taken us the long way. My friends were furious and ready to mutiny when I pulled over in the farmer's field. It was a hot, overcast day. I suggested we find the Cadillac that corresponded to the year of our birth and carve our initials into it. John, and Dean enthusiastically embraced the idea and we set out to find our Cadillac. The cars, baked in the Texas sun burned our hands.

Duff and Donnie just leaned against the Camaro and glared daggers at us.

They eventually decided to join us when we struck up a conversation with a hunky young man. He was a pale bare-chested boy from Canada with a camera. He told me he was a photographer. He was touring old route 66.

"You look like a cowboy," he told me. "Would you pose for me?"

My friends laughed. I was wearing Sperry Top-Siders.

He had me put on my cowboy hat and ride the Cadillac like it was a horse, "Now, do it nude."

None of my friends spoke to me for the next two hours.

As an olive branch, I let Donnie drive and I rode on the transmission hump. Duff had swiped the pillow that Donnie usually sat on and put it behind his head. My bony ass was riding on only the carpeted metal. Dean moved his knees so I that I had nothing to rest my back on.

"Spreading your legs already?" I challenged.

In solidarity, Donnie gunned the accelerator, I almost tumbled into the backseat. I was outnumbered.

Donnie purposefully hit every bump to pound my ass.

"Go ahead, Donnie. Blow a tire. You're the one who took out the spare and left it in California!" I bellowed, triumphant. We were at an impasse. I should not have had the last word.

It would be a long drive to Dallas. I hated myself as much as my friends hated me.

I put on a cassette from our favorite film. We must have watched this VHS a hundred times, we knew all the dialogue by heart.

Stevie B was never able to resist Bette Midler's monologue from *The Rose*, "*Oh Honey, I can smell another woman at five hundred paces,*" Stevie B mimicked word for word. "*And that's an easy one to catch!*"

Even Duff joined in, "*So what do you do when he comes home with the smell of another woman on his person?*"

Donnie jumps ahead, "*Oh, honey let me open up my loving arms and my loving legs, dive right in, baby the water is fine.*"

By the time Bette Midler catches up my friends are all laughing and they've forgotten they hate me as I add my voice, *"Pack your bags! I'm putting on my little waitress cap and my fancy high heeled shoes. I'm gonna find me a real man, a good man. A true man. A man to love me for sure."*

It was getting dark by the time we pulled into Dallas. Donnie headed straight for the gay bar. I considered suggesting we find a motel to stay first, but kept my mouth shut, not wanting to upset the delicate peace we'd achieved.

Looking For Love In All The Wrong Places
CHAPTER 11

Johnny Lee's song from *Urban Cowboy* was playing on all the jukeboxes across the country that year. It was the only country song we knew.

"Searching their eyes, looking for traces of what I'm dreaming of."

We blew into JR's gay bar with great expectations. We were accustomed to our arrival at a gay bar being greeted with great fanfare. Back home, fans would scream our names. Velvet ropes would part. Drinks and drugs would be pressed into our hands. Here, nobody bothered to look up from their beers.

We were windblown and disheveled from eight hours in a convertible. The Texans at JRs had made the effort to look nice. Their boots were freshly polished, and their shirts were crisply ironed.

"Good lord, that one even ironed her Wranglers!" John said, the first bitchy words out of his mouth.

"Just like Bucky!" I couldn't resist a dig at the new kid horning into our line up at West Street Beach.

Bucky looked like a missing Kennedy. He was a preppy from Buck's County PA. I didn't think he was line-up material.

"He irons his boardshorts," was my main complaint.

While we were on this road trip, RD let him sit on our spots at the beach.

The only effort we made was to pop the collar up on our polo shirts. I knew we should have found a motel room first and freshened up.

Nobody rushed to buy us a drink. We hadn't accounted for that.

"How much does a drink even cost?" Duff wondered.

We elbowed our way to the bar, unsure of how to do this.

"Eeew!" Donnie pinched his nose closed. All the cowboys had doused themselves with cologne. "It smells like RD in here."

RD was our young friend who aspired to be an old queen and would daub himself with half a bottle of Santos by Cartier before a night out.

"Six shots of Cuervo" Stevie B called out.

I had hoped he had Jim Moniz' Credit Card to put it on. He didn't.

"What kind of Sugar Baby are you? Without Daddy's credit card." We grudgingly fished out some dollars from our pockets.

"We need 3 more!" Dean said, "For the tip!"

Duff and Dean broke away and moved hand and hand through the crowd to no effect. Latino men approached Steve Bernal expecting him to *Se Habla Español*. I got in line to ride the mechanical bull.

"That ain't no Cadillac," Donnie hissed. "Best keep your clothes on bitch!"

His snide remark brought a little attention my way. I noticed several men looking at me from under their cowboy hats as I mounted the bull to do my best Debra Winger. I was tossed off after a few seconds. My friends were laughing and pointing. I stood up with as much dignity as I could muster. After all, I had just come from a modeling assignment in Amarillo. The bull operator swung the bull around and knocked me back on my ass.

"This place sucks," Duff and Dean reported back. "Wait till you see the dance floor!"

We agreed we could afford another shot of tequila. Newly fortified I expected to throw myself with abandon onto the dance floor. Once we started to dance to Donna Summer's *Bad Girls* and took our shirts off, I was sure we wouldn't have to pay for another drink.

I was so wrong. There was no Donna Summer blaring.

"Are you sure this is a gay bar?" Duff harrumphed.

Instead, couples were dancing together in pairs like at a cousin's wedding, to country music.

I was startled to hear a deep voice ask me, "Care to dance?"

I shook my head no as a giant black man led me by the hand.

"It's impolite to refuse a dance when you're standing on the edge of the dance floor."

"I don't know how to country dance," I sputtered.

He took my hand in his and pulled me close at the small of my back and began dancing me backwards.

"Slow, Slow, Quick, Quick, Slow." He taught me to two-step.

He was gliding in his cowboy boots. I kept getting tangled up in my flip flops. I kicked them off and danced barefoot.

"You've got delicious feet," he said shocking me. The tempo picked up and we were circling the dance floor with the other couples. I was getting the hang of this. Now, I *was* Debra Winger.

Soon, he was spinning me around. This was fun. This was romantic. We talked while we danced. He was a baggage handler at DFW.

"I could use my free flight to visit you in California."

I looked for my friends as I was in over my head. The song ended and I tried to break away. Strong, he pulled me in for a kiss. I had never had to tilt my head up to kiss someone. I was used to being the taller man.

Duff and Donnie caught the kiss and came over to separate us as if they were the Georgia Patrol. They sequestered me in a corner for the interrogation.

"Can we stay with him?"

Turns out they spent the motel money buying more drinks. They pushed me to dance with the man again. He told me his name was Mr. Johnson. He was very formal. He seemed a little distant.

"I live with my momma and my sisters," he answered.

He kissed me again. His tongue was as big as a Porterhouse steak.

"How long are you in town?" he asked coming up for air.

"We're just passing through."

"I don't know where we are staying." I kissed him goodbye.

"Your feet really turn me on."

"Thanks." I didn't know the appropriate reply. I went searching for my flip flops.

"Well?" Donnie confronted me.

I shook my head no. We didn't have a place to sleep tonight.

"What are we gonna do?"

Get Down Tonight | CHAPTER 12

At a loss for where to stay, I grabbed one of the gay rags that were always piled at a gay bar. I thumbed through the pages of 976 ads, wondering what to do.

Then I found it, tonight was 18+ night at the Midtowne Spa. Rooms were half price (membership not included)! For only $5.00 each we got a private room at the gay bathhouse. I already had a membership from the LA branch. I knew most of us did. Duff spent the extra money to buy a temporary membership so that Dean wouldn't know he already had one.

I never got the hang of the rules for being gay. It was acceptable to sleep with every newcomer on the beach, but a bathhouse card made you trash. Donnie too, pretended he didn't have a card, so he paid extra so that John would think he was a virgin. Unashamed, John from Santa Barbara laid his card with his cash, like he was playing a trump card in Euchre.

These private rooms weren't meant for sleeping. They had a twin mattress and a pillow. They had a TV with porn playing. Unlike JRs bar, this place played disco music, unfortuately. I could feel the bass thump vibrating my bed. I put the pillow over my head to drown out Vicki Sue Robinson. It was impossible to sleep. Who's idiotic idea was this? The sheets stank of bleach (which was comforting). The mattress was wrapped in plastic and the sheets kept slipping off. I wasn't drunk enough to pass out drunk. If only I had a Quaalude. After all, they were prescribed as a sleep aid. I had always been able to find a Quaalude at a bathhouse. Once in New York City, I found too many of them and was discovered passed out on the shower floor at the St. Mark's Baths.

Guys I had seen on the beach (Lee Ryder and Leo Ford) were doing it doggy style on the TV.

I wrapped a towel around my waist and decided to take a hot shower. The corridors outside the room were painted black and they were pitch dark. The communal showers were open to the hallway. Passersby stopped to take in the show. I knew I looked good wet. I felt like Jennifer Beals in Flashdance, the shower spray bouncing off my volleyball player's body.

I purposely dropped the soap.

"Lord Have Mercy!" I heard over the splash of the water, "that white ass is Dee-lish-ous."

Satisfied, I ended the show and headed back to my room. Certain that I had a line of men following me, I took a circuitous route, so they didn't know where my room was.

"Hey, Kid!" a man called. "Wait up I have a present for you!"

"This ain't my first time at the rodeo," I retorted.

"You coulda fooled me, the way you fell off my bull." The man laughed a condescending laugh.

I was certain he was the mechanical bull operator from JRs. I wasn't going to turn around and let him humiliate me again.

"Want a lude?" This got my attention. "A peace offering."

I turned to face my tormentor.

"I'm sorry," he said handing me two Quaaludes. "I just couldn't resist," he said with a shit-eating grin. "The bigger they are, the harder they fall," he laughed. He was missing a tooth. He was short, shorter than Donnie. He looked like a Centaur. From the waist up he looked like a kid, hairless torso, pale skin, skinny arms—a twink. From the waist down he was all man. Powerful legs covered in dark hair. A perfectly shaped rutabega that could have won the Blue Ribbon at the county fair. Big bunioned feet. I was beginning to understand my black cowboy's obsession with my feet. A lifetime squeezed into Tony Lamas must deform a Texan's foot.

"Why don't ya take those Ludes and see how long you can stay on this time!"

He steered me towards a water fountain like he was two-stepping me around a dance floor. Mindful of the St. Mark's Baths, I only took one.

"Girl what are you taking?" Duff accosted me as he came round a corner. "Got one for your sister?"

I didn't understand what Duff was doing. He never talked camp. He never flounced, except for that one time we sang Memory from Cats, "I was beautiful then."

I made the introductions, "This is my friend Duff, we're from Laguna Beach, we're on a road trip to Miami."

Even though I had another Quaalude still in my hand, I thought I could pimp Duff off and get another one out of the Centaur. Since, I wasn't a catcher and Duff was he could ride the bull and be the one to see how long he can stay on. My plan worked. I was able to sneak back to my room alone.

Quaaludes were a marvelous drug. First your fingers would start to tingle and your body went to jelly. Then you fell in love with whomever was next to you.

"Hey Dave," I was startled to hear my name.

Nobody knew me in Dallas. I recognized the way that deep bass voice resonated through my body. Without turning around, I waited for who I knew was my big black cowboy.

"Fancy meeting you here." Melting into my quaalude, I let myself fall back into his arms.

Then he did something to me that nobody had ever done before. He picked me up and carried me in his arms like a baby. Once again, I was Debra Winger, but this time in *An Officer and a Gentleman.*

"Those beautiful bare feet should never touch this nasty floor." He removed my towel and put me to bed. "You are a white boy," he exclaimed looking at my untanned butt. He gave me a gentle kiss, his lips were so plush and pillowy. Soon his Porterhouse Steak of a tongue was in my panting mouth. Then it made a beeline to my toes. He was the only man able to resist a detour to take my boyhood into his mouth. He was more interested in my feet.

"What's your name?" I asked, breaking the first rule of the tubs.

"I done told you already, call me Mr. Johnson."

I fell into a deep sleep while this stranger massaged my feet. I dreamt I heard Dean honking "Hon," in the corridor.

In the morning, I was the one calling for Duff in the corridors. I couldn't find any of my friends. These rooms were not intended for overnight sleepers. The time limit for a room was 8 hours.

The manager interrupted Donna Summer and would announce that, "Room 224, it's time to Check Out."

Passed out on a Quaalude, I awoke to a pounding on my door. The attendant was halfway in the room before I was out of bed. Hurriedly, I went to stand up and my feet flew out from under me, I landed on my ass.

"Dios Mio!" The attendant came back with a manager.

I was looking at the smear of semen under my feet, and I understood exactly what had happened. Mr. Johnson had his wicked way with the soles of my feet.

Fearing a lawsuit, the manager closely examined the floor where I slipped and fell. "Is this yours?" He asked picking up the second Quaalude and holding it in front of me.

I held out my hand for it.

He shook his head no without giving it to me, "Yes or No? Is this pill yours?"

Bathhouse managers are difficult old queens. It's a thankless job.

"Come with me," he said leading me through the now empty corridors. In his tiny office he gave me the Quaalude after I signed a release stating I wouldn't hold the club accountable for my slip and fall. Outside his window I saw my friends sitting at a table. He gave me a free membership card and bid me good day.

I joined my friends who were all freshly showered and eating the complimentary waffles from the waffle bar. I couldn't imagine eating in a sex club. I'm wary of finding hairs in even the finest restaurants. I couldn't look at Duff, nor he, I.

Donnie was the only one conversing. "I ran into your black cowboy." He crowed.

This got everyone's attention.

Duff only cocked an eyebrow. "It's Twue, it's Twue," he said mimicking Madeline Kahn from one of our favorite movie, Mel Brooks *Blazing Saddles*. We spent many nights back in Laguna watching Mel Brooks Movies in Jim Moniz's screening room.

"What do you want to do today?" I asked.

We had the entire day free, as we weren't supposed to be in New Orleans until late tomorrow. Cranky, nobody seemed interested in staying in Dallas another night. It was only 7:00 AM and already sweltering in the Texas humidity.

"I want to go to Neiman Marcus," said Stevie B, who must secretly have Jim Moniz credit card. I wanted to show my friends the view from Reunion Tower at the Hyatt Regency. I was still young enough to get a thrill riding the glass elevators through the atrium and then up the outside of the tower. Plus, it was free. And we should see the Grassy Knoll since we were in Dallas.

"I don't care what we do, I'm not staying in a bathhouse another night." Dean put his foot down.

"Me Neither," Seconded Stevie B.

"Well, I just got a free year's membership." I explained the circumstances, which took the wind out of Donnie' sails.

The boys went out to the car to pick the day's outfits, I showered up and joined them in the parking lot. They were squabbling over the polo shirts in Stevie B's suitcase. Thoughtfully, Donnie was holding my loose trunk lid so that it didn't break off. Donnie could afford to as he had his own polos in size small. Five of us had to share the mediums. I switched yesterday's boardshorts for a clean pair. And I got the last clean Polo shirt, in the ugliest color. The turquoise shirt clashed with my red boardshorts, so I dropped trou again and put on my gray pair of corded Quiksilvers. Quiks were 2" shorter than OPs, which could be dangerous when you go commando without underwear.

Between the six of us I don't think we brought one pair of underwear.

Turn The Beat Around | CHAPTER 13

It was easy to find Neiman Marcus, Dallas had street signs directing you to its major attractions. But Neiman's didn't open until 11:00 AM. It was only 7:30 AM. We had time to kill, so I drove us to the Grassy Knoll where JFK was shot supposedly by Lee Harvey Oswald.

Being the last of the Baby Boomers, JFK's assassination was a defining moment for our generation. I was obsessed with Jim Garrison's book discrediting the Lone Gunman Theory. See, I was learning something in college. I was captivated by the homosexual Clay Shaw—who knew a decorator could be so deadly? (I knew having spent summers on West Street). We saw the grassy knoll and the Texas School Book Depository before 9:00 AM. Still 2 hours until Neiman's opens. I drove us to Reunion Tower. It was easy to find as it dominated the Dallas skyline.

Free parking was less easy to find, as the Hyatt Hotel was charging. I pulled into valet parking for 2 reasons, the valet was cute and I sensed a mutiny if I circled the block another time.

"Are y'all from California?" The valet parker excitedly asked. "I've always wanted to go there! I'll leave your car out front."

I instantly fell in love, "One of y'all is walking home, I've got a new boyfriend." I said loud enough for the valet to hear.

This was a stupid thing to say.

"Suit yourself, I am tired of you all." Dean said, unable to get the Texas Y'all correct.

The boys continued to grumble all the way to the elevators. Hyatt Regency Hotels were the epitome of modern design in the 1970's. Architect John Portman created a soaring atrium lobby with cantilevered floors that hung over each other. (At least until they collapsed as they did in Kansas City, killing hundreds.)

"It's just like *The Towering Inferno*." Donnie said in awe looking at the jewel like glass elevators.

I had never experienced vertigo before. I had to drop to all fours as the elevator rocketed out of the atrium and was ascending freely attached to the side of the tower.

"Didn't you spend last night like that?" Donnie said, oblivious to my distress.

"You're the one who insisted we do this!" Duff needled me.

Everyone enjoyed my discomfort as I crawled out of the elevator on my hands and knees. The Observation Deck was no relief. I could not bring myself to stand up. The spectacular view of the Dallas skyline went unappreciated by me.

I had balled myself up against the outside wall of the revolving restaurant on the verge of nausea.

"Let's go inside" Donnie said to my relief.

Once inside I was able to stand back up on my feet.

"Hon, can we get the brunch buffet?"

Everyone was excited to spend more money. By now I had broken out in a cold sweat. At the hostess station in the center of the room, we got the reception we were accustomed to. The three beautiful black hostesses fussed over us and escorted us to the best table.

"Where y'all from?"

"Are y'all movie stars?"

"Y'all so cute in your matching polo shirts."

I couldn't tell if they were making fun of us. I was relieved to find the all you can eat brunch was under $10.00 with free champagne. I could feel the vertigo coming back when I noticed the restaurant was revolving. After a few sips of champagne, my stomach settled. I was able to appreciate the view. My friends were having a gay old time. They began rehashing last night.

"Did you do it with the black cowboy?" Donnie challenged.

"No," I said which was technically true. "Mr. Johnson was a perfect gentleman."

Stevie B broke into song, *"Mrs. Johnson you been wearing your dresses way to high. It's been reported you've been drinking and a runnin' round with men and going wild."*

All my friends sang the chorus of *Harper Valley PTA*. I was afraid we were getting out of hand. Every time we revolved past the hostess stand the three black girls would giggle and point. The other diners had taken the occasion to dress up. We were in shorts and polo shirts. Most looked to be tourists. One table with bejeweled Dallas matrons with towering bouffants looked to be locals. I was concerned about offending them when talk turned back to the bathhouse.

"Did you find the swimming pool?" Stevie B asked.

"Everything is bigger in Texas," he exclaimed.

"How many did you have?" Duff asked.

Stevie B shook his head no.

"*Oh, get off it!*" Duff mimicked Nurse Diesel in *High Anxiety*, "*I know you better than you know yourself.*"

This brought us to tears.

"*You do not get fruit cup.*"

We caught our breath, the hostesses were still laughing. I wondered if they were the sisters Mr. Johnson spoke of.

"Did you see the troll train Donnie had going?"

Callow youth, we prided ourselves on the number of guys we could get to follow us through the tubs hoping they might get lucky. This conga line that snaked through the corridors of the bath house looked like a train, especially when it came to an intersection. Duff held the record at 20.

"Shhh," I shushed.

Our Table revolved past the Dallas matrons again.

"Flo would kill for that hair," Donnie said, pointing.

Flo was the drag queen who cut the ribbon on Memorial Day. I was mortified. John from Santa Barbara excused himself to use the restroom. The hostesses were still laughing. Stevie B looked at the new digital watch Jim Moniz had gifted him.

"Neimans opens in a half hour."

"Dave," John comes back, his mouth aghast.

"The hostesses are laughing because you are flashing them every time we revolve past."

I tuck my junk back into my Quiksilvers, "OK, let's go to Neiman's now," I say hoping to make a quick escape.

"Young Man," the bouffant matron calls to me, "Neiman Marcus doesn't open until noon in the summertime. No need to rush."

My stomach sinks, dear lord, she's heard everything we've said.

"Are you young men visiting?" She coos, "May we ask from where you hail?"

"Yes, you May, M'aam," Duff turns on the charm, his green eyes glittering. "We are from Laguna Beach, California."

I can see Duff has the ladies captivated.

"What brings you to our fair city?"

"We're just passing through, on a road trip to Miami."

Although I am answering the ladies are still looking at Duff.

"Are you in a hurry?" She asks.

I'm trying to calculate the right answer to avoid being set up with a daughter.

"Not really," Duff answers, "we are supposed to meet a friend from Laguna Beach tomorrow in New Orleans."

"You must see our beaches." She says, "Is it possible to arrive in New Orleans in the evening?"

Duff nods his pretty head, his glossy hair shimmering.

"Then that settles it." She glances at her lunch companions. "I insist you boys stay at my beach house in Galveston. I'll ring my house boy and have him open up the house."

With the wave of a bejeweled finger, a phone is brought to their table. She must have sensed our hesitation.

"You'll be doing me the favor. The house has been closed up all winter."

I'm sad to say, I don't remember this generous lady's name. I remember it once being in my address book—I sent her a thank you card. I burned that address book after I buried all the names in it.

"You boys are a breath of fresh air. The house will be the better for it. Riccardo will prepare a late supper." We put handfuls of crumpled dollar bills on the table to cover the check. And yet, the lady didn't rescind her invitation.

Magic | CHAPTER 14

Giddy with excitement and tipsy on champagne, the six of us popped out of the Hyatt Regency crooning the Glen Campbell hit, *"I still hear your sea winds blowin'."*

As promised, my Camaro was parked In front of the hotel among an ostentation of Rolls Royces.

The cute valet was grinning at us, "I hope you don't mind, I put your top up to keep the seats from burning you."

I fished a five-dollar bill from my pocket, remembering how good it felt to get a big tip. (This was my lunch money for a week. It would have bought five Quarter Pounders—<u>with</u> cheese.) He didn't notice the denomination of my bill.

Duff was bending over showing off his ass, "I know, look how they burned my thighs!"

My Camaro's seats were black vinyl. They got as hot as a branding iron. I took advantage of the convertible top being up to spread out my road map on the roof.

"Where are you going next?" the valet was pressed next to me, looking at my map.

He was as excited as I was (about our travels). He was so close to me I could smell his Juicy Fruit (gum). I was in love (again). He had pale blue eyes, pale pink lips and a dusting of freckles across his nose.

"We're headed to Galveston" Duff stole my thunder.

"I know the way!" the valet turned to me bubbling with excitement.

I thought he was going to kiss me. Instead, he draped his arm across my shoulder, and he showed me the route we should take.

He whispered, "My family has a summer house there."

This was the first time I recognized the synchronicity of the universe, which was to stay with me the entirety of my life.

"I have a feeling that your house is where we are staying!" I showed him the address scribbled on a napkin.

"I see you met Mother!" He gave me a big hug that lifted my feet off the ground.

"You should come with us!"

His blue eyes looked deep into my soul, "I can't."

I gave him another hug, "Tell your mom we met. And tell her thanks."

His name was Toby.

Lovesick, I drove towards Neiman Marcus. They were about to open a new branch in Newport Beach at Fashion Island. We'd have bragging rights on the beach, "Oh, we just came back from the flagship in Dallas."

In 1981, GQ was the bible on West Street Beach. Every month the magazine's new issue would be passed breathlessly from towel to towel. Bruce Weber had just made his name shooting the covers. The homosexual ascetic was on newsstands across America. We thought GQ stood for Gays and Queers. Weber fetishized athleticism. One summer, Pepperdine swimmer Jeff Aquilon took your breath away.

Natural, athletic bodies were the ideal. We had ours from playing volleyball and swimming to yachts.

We strode into this luxury citadel with confidence, despite not having a penny in our pocket. In our polo shirts and shorts, we felt like undiscovered cover boys.

"Perhaps you boys would like something in our Cruise Collection."

How dare he! I thought. Clearly I did not understand Cruising was something other than looking for dick in a rest stop.

The salesman's beautiful suit and perfect haircut intimidated me. I was always wary of older gay men.

"We're just window shopping," Duff stops me with an elbow in the ribs.

We were ushered out of the bespoke suit collection with its perfectly arranged silk ties in their own wooden cubby. Now we were in the Ralph Lauren boutique. The salesman snapped his fingers over his head and held up six. Champagne was soon poured. We weren't even asked for ID. Every color of that season's

Polo shirts were displayed as it they were in an advertisement. (In our car's trunk we had almost every one of them.) Beside this was Ralph Lauren's newest line Chaps.

The salesman toasted us with his own glass of champagne, "Did Daddy give you a limit?"

I was offended that he assumed we were all kept boys like Stevie B. My friends shake their head "no," like Fosse dancers. This led to another round of champagne. I had to hand it to my friends.

"Perhaps you will find Mr. Lauren's new collection to your liking: The Double R."

The salesman caught me peeking at the price tag. $200 for a pair of jeans. He excused himself.

"It's five hours to Galveston."

We exited through the perfume aisle, searching for a place to leave our flutes. I asked for a sample vial of Lauren by Ralph Lauren. This smelled of gardenia and reminded me of a girl I had a summer romance with.

"Oh, Camille!" Duff recognized the scent.

Hot humid air assaulted us as we went through the revolving doors—twice—we had never encountered these before. The car was so hot that a cassette tape had melted in the player. It was bent in half dripping like wax.

"That's OK," Donnie says, "it was just the Manhattan Transfer." His least favorite.

We put the top down and headed out of Dallas towards Galveston.

Stevie B requests the Damron Guide from the glovebox, "There are two gay bars in Galveston." He reports back, "Tell me they play disco."

"Jeezus John." Donnie screams "Did you pinch that tie?"

John from Santa Barbara had a new silk tie flapping about his bare chest in the windblown convertible. I am reminded of how little we know about each other. And how little we cared.

We are blissfully driving to a stranger's house with a thief in the backseat.

I never knew John's last name.

The rolling hills reminded me of the roller coaster that was Coast Highway through Laguna. I wondered what we are missing on West Street beach.

Revolving doors are not the only unfamiliar thing in Texas. With a thunderclap we are caught in a sudden downpour.

The boy's shriek like debutantes. The top slowly whirrs up with the flick of a switch. We are soaking wet. Most of us Californians, we had never before seen a summer storm. It was a beautiful lightning show until the windows fogged up. I couldn't see the road in front of me. I had to turn on the defroster.

"It's too hot, turn it off"."

"Roll the fucking windows down."

"It smells like JRs in here!" My friends must have sampled all the Nieman Marcus' colognes.

This was the first complaint of the day. We had our mojo back. Magical things happened when we were together, like a coven of witches. If only, our empty gas tank might magically fill up. We were running on empty on a lonely country road.

The rain finally stopped. A double rainbow appeared. 18 wheelers blocked an intersection.

"I've got to pee," was Donnie's Pavlovian response to the truckers.

As if we've conjured it up there is a service plaza up ahead. I collect gas money from my friends, being careful that John doesn't see where I hide mine. I hand over $10 for pump #18.

"Fill her up," a man behind me says.

I dream of being an adult and one day able to afford to fill up a gas tank. As I Squeegee the bugs off the windshield, I notice the appreciative looks we get from other travelers.

A smiling man approaches me, "We piled in cars like that before the war," he said, extending his hand.

I reached out to shake it.

"I wanted to use the Squeegee," he said, confused. That was typical me, gliding through the world thinking I was a celebrity.

"Are you done signing autographs?" Duff doesn't miss a thing. I'm sure he will never let me forget this.

"I'm waiting on the pump to stop." It's way past the $10 and quickly approaching $20. I reach to stop the pump.

"Don't." I hear Duff's voice.

The pump stops at $25.00.

When I fire up the Camaro it has a full tank. Maybe we are witches? The man behind me must have confused the clerk when he said, "filler up." Or, did he treat us?

It's a pleasant drive on country roads to Galveston. Everyone is content. The rain cooled things down. McDonald's was running a bogo on Quarter Pounders. Donnie shared his with me.

Galveston, Oh Galveston | CHAPTER 15

We pull into Galveston under a setting sun. Seagulls flew over swampland. Toby's mom's beach house was a white shingled Victorian home. Coming from the land of tract houses, this old house looks like a wedding cake. It's very grand.

With a warm welcome, the houseman introduces himself as Riccardo, from Cuba. We swoon.

"You don't look like a serial killer," Dean says apropos of nothing. Riccardo insists on carrying our bags. I think he is just showing off. Muscles bulge through his white linen shirt as he carries the bags upstairs.

"Madame apologizes you won't each have your own room."

This starts us giggling which won't stop until we depart Galveston. "Madame," makes us picture Waylon Flowers and his puppet, Madame. Along with Paul Lynde, these are the only representations of homosexuals on TV.

"Imagine Madame the puppet in madame's Texas bouffant," Duff whispers to me. I cackle like Paul Lynde.

"I'm gonna pee," Duff is laughing so hard. I flash to the time Donnie came flying down the stairs of our condo in Dana Point.

"Don't you dare!" Donnie screamed from upstairs in his butchest voice. I am in tears remembering this. The houseman doesn't know what to make of us hyenas. Camille's friend Joey Coons was crashing on our living room floor after a party.

He was begging his trick, "Pee on Me!"

Like a witch Donnie flew downstairs to stop it, "Don't you dare!" He threw himself in front of the man's open fly.

We couldn't stifle our hysterics as Riccardo detailed the house rules.

"Only three squares of TP," First Donnie giggled, then Duff did, Stevie B pulled me to the floor with a guffaw.

We were still young enough that potty humor slayed us.

Riccardo was losing his patience, "This is an historic Queen Anne home and the plumbing is very sensitive."

"Just like Donnie."

Riccardo left us rolling around on the floor in hysterics.

"Dinner will be served at 9:00," he leaves us. "No need to dress as Madame is not in residence."

Picturing a naked dinner party put us in convulsions. Like hiccups we couldn't stop. I took a cold shower which worked. I managed to find a clean polo shirt without breaking down into laughter. I pictured Daisy Buchanan tossing them like Gatsby's.

"*Have you ever seen such beautiful shirts?*" Because this didn't make me laugh, I thought I was safe. But.

Duff was breathing into a paper bag. I lost it when i read the grocery store's name, Piggly Wiggly. I had to slap my face to keep from exploding in laughter. Reminding me of Donnie's Ranchero, him imitating Faye Dunaway. "It's a car and a truck!" ("she's my daughter and my sister") I took a deep breath determined to marshall all the dignity I could. The dining table was exquisitely set with Crystal and silver. Yes, I flicked my finger against a goblet to hear it ring.

I found Stevie B resting his chin on his wrist and gazing up at Riccardo with his big brown eyes. Riccardo stirred a steaming pot. Son of a Bitch. I was so angry at Stevie B. This stopped my laughter.

I didn't think it was fair for boys who had a boyfriend to go after a second one when I was still single.

Riccardo was undeniably sexy with his bulging biceps and lupine eyes, and I had heard about the size of Cuban Sugar Cane (another root vegetable).

I was not about to let somebody have him if I couldn't. Like your typical suburban murder-suicide.

"Hey, Steve, What's the name of that bar you wanted to go to?" Stevie—B lifts his chin from his hand and shoots me the finger. I regroup, "Maybe Riccardo knows it," I'm dangerously close to outing us. If my gaydar was malfunctioning, Riccardo might kill us in a case of gay panic. Dan White had just assassinated Harvey Milk in San Francisco. He had only been slapped on the wrist with a misdemeanor using the Twinkie Defense. If we live, I doubt madame's hospitality extends to homosexuals. "I don't care what they do in their own home, but I wouldn't have one in mine." I'd heard many times visiting aunts.

The arrival of Duff and Dean saved my ass. But only for a minute. "Hon, look at this lamp, I want one for our bedroom."

I steal a glance at Riccardo, he doesn't bat an eye.

But, Stevie B is batting his big cow eyes at Riccardo.

I go for the jugular, "What time are we supposed to meet your Sugar Daddy tomorrow?"

Vanquished Stevie B gets up to wring my neck. Before I can snag his seat, Duff has swanned over and sat down. I take satisfaction that he is sitting on his best feature. Duff is summoning all the power in the room to illuminate his green eyes.

"You'll blow the circuits, imagine how brittle the wiring is if we can only use 3 squares of TP." I stifle a chuckle, imagining the outlets sparking and the sconces flickering like in a haunted house.

Duff's eyes have distracted Riccardo, his pot is bubbling. I wonder what's for dinner. My palette is unsophisticated, I don't recognize the smell. I'm a very picky eater. I begin to worry that I will go to bed hungry. In more ways than one.

"Hon, come here," Dean calls.

I needn't have worried. Watching Duff pretend to admire the crystal, I miss Donnie break away from John and steal the seat near Riccardo. This will not stand.

"Donnie," I admonish.

I'm at a loss, both Donnie and Riccardo turn to look at me. I can feel Stevie B and Duff rooting for me to choke.

"What would Madame think…"

I knew I could send us all into fits. Riccardo has his eyebrow cocked towards me, daring me to finish.

"Of us disturbing her chef and expecting him to entertain us while he is cooking." I saved my own ass. And shot it as well. I couldn't very well take a seat and chat him up now. Riccardo gets the last word. Without saying a thing.

He lifts the hem of his shirt to mop his perspiring brow, revealing a taut stomach tantalizingly accented with a treasure trail of dark hair. We all fall silent, imagining the buried treasure.

The only sound to be heard was the bubbling of the pot and the creaking of the old house as it settles in the cool night air. I decide that it would be vulgar to dally with the help when I'm in love with the master of the house, Toby.

Only John from Santa Barbara was unfazed by the display of pulchritude. He breaks the silence, "What is this?" he asks picking up a piece of crystal art from the mantle.

"It is a turtle," Riccardo says in an unamused voice.

"Please put it down." I watch John from Santa Barbara to make sure he doesn't pocket it.

"Madame collects Lalique." We are all too afraid to giggle. Riccardo has had enough of us. "Should you wish to send madame a hostess gift, she is registered at Neiman's."

Chastened, we took our seats silently. With a white napkin draped over his nut brown forearm, Riccardo approached me. I don't know why he chose me to present the evening's wine selection. I suspected he was intent on embarrassing me as revenge for my cock blocking him. I knew nothing about wine. I had no idea what to do. Should my napkin already be on my lap?

As if reading my mind, Riccardo places the napkin unobtrusively on my lap. Did his pinkie purposely graze my inner thigh? My teenage dick now tents the linen napkin. My confidence restored, I negotiated the wine presentation expertly, nodding affirmatively that he may pour. I was hypnotized by the pulsing vein in his forearm as it snaked under the napkin on his arm and resurfaced on his bicep.

I recall that Madame only serves a buttery Chardonnay with She-Crab soup, never an oaky one. This was a California Chardonnay. Far Niente always reminds me of this unforgettable meal. I wish I could remember Madame's name. I've never forgotten this night and I better understand Tennessee Williams, "The kindness of Strangers."

Thank you, Toby's mom for expanding my palette.

Donnie McPhedran | CHAPTER 16

When I think about Donnie McPhedran, I hear a ditty Sandra Bernhard wrote for an ex-girlfriend:

She's a tumbling tumbleweed,
She's a tumbling tumbleweed,
she was born from a tumbleweed seed,
round and around and around she goes.
Where she stops nobody knows.
Nobody knows.

Like a tumbleweed, Donnie McPhedran blew out of Bisbee, Arizona in 1977.

He came to a stop in Laguna Beach, California, which is where I met him.

I assumed he was my age of 18. Donnie was a pocket-sized cowboy, today we would consider him a twink. But twinks don't drive a 1971 429 Cobra Jet Ranchero with a Hurst 4-speed stick shift.

My friend Duff Paddock brought him to the Hotel Laguna where we both worked as valet parkers.

I'm guessing Duff was hitchhiking on the Coast Highway in our uniform of tiny white tennis shorts and a polo shirt.

Duff had an ass that could stop traffic.

Which came in handy when you were hitch-hiking to work and running late.

I recognized the look of disappointment in Donnie's eyes when he realized that Duff was handing him off to me, Duff having gotten the ride to work that he was looking for.

I wanted to look Donnie's car over and figured it would give me a chance to look him over as well. Donnie's entire face lit up when I asked him to show me his car. Donnie had an exuberant, guileless face. He could never disguise his emotions. Right now, he looked like a rescue dog at the ASPCA wagging his tail for his next prospective master. It didn't appear that he cared who took him home. He just wanted love and affection. And was eager to offer the same in return.

"Show me your car." I said, and quickly amended, "truck."

The Ford Ranchero, like the Chevy El Camino, was both a car and a truck.

At this Donnie began slapping his face like the infamous scene with Faye Dunaway in the movie *Chinatown*.

"She's a car," slap

"She's a truck," slap.

"She's my sister and my daughter."

I fell in love with Donnie in that moment. I was curious how this teenage cowboy was aware of this camp classic movie scene.

"Lemme hear that Cobra Jet 429!" I asked Donnie to start her up.

I could feel the rumble of that big block V8 in my balls. The hood scoop shook like a vibrator through the hood

"How do you resist the urge to sit on that?" pointing to the throbbing hood scoop. Ford, like Dodge, offered a shaker hood scoop on their muscle cars.

A shaker hood scoop was mounted directly to the engine on top of the air filter and protruded through a cut out in the hood, to suck in clean, cool air.

"Just like a glory hole," Donnie said as he closed the hood, and the big black scoop penetrated the hole in the hood.

Because the scoop was attached to the engine, it shook when the motor did. That's why it was called the shaker.

Donnie noticed my excitement in my white tennis shorts.

"Wanna go for a ride?" He asked adjusting the bulge in his Wranglers.

I didn't clock off my shift, or tell Duff I was leaving. I'm sure he realized when he heard Donnie drop the clutch and peel out onto the Coast Highway. Laying a patch of rubber halfway up the hill, I remember worrying that a customer might think we were hot rodding their cars.

"Is everything OK?" Donnie asked.

This is the first time I noticed his empathy. Before I could share my teenage angst about my job, Donnie hit the brakes leaving another patch of rubber on Coast Highway.

"Wanna lift?" he asked the bare-chested hitch-hiker on the curb.

The kid tossed his surfboard in the truck bed and I slid over on the bench seat next to Donnie. I knocked the Hurst shifter out of gear with my long legs. Donnie had the seat up close since he was short. I got out and let the wet kid get in the middle.

"I'm going to Salt Creek," he said.

"I have a condo off Green Lantern," Donnie replied.

I knew both locations were next to each other in nearby Dana Point. Donnie was a good driver. He maneuvered that beast of a car/truck, expertly through the roller coaster dips of Coast Highway in South Laguna. When you ordered a Cobra Jet 429 engine in the Ranchero there was no room under the hood for a power steering pump. Still, Donnie was able to muscle the steering wheel one-handed while he shifted the gears with his other hand. Being a good driver was just one of my many requirements to be considered boyfriend material.

I watched the Hurst T handle graze the surfer's bare inner thighs as Donnie went through the gears. Donnie's eyes caught mine in the rearview mirror as we passed Salt Creek Beach. I'd been in California long enough to know to keep quiet. Donnie didn't want me to point out we were passing the hitch-hiker's destination. Donnie kept the car in fourth, the shifter and Donnie's hand was buried in the kid's crotch like the horn of a saddle.

It was a beautiful, sunny California day. Once we were in the Jacuzzi I began to worry about getting back to work.

"Want a lude?" Donnie offered.

The kid swallowed his and Donnie swallowed the kid. I realized neither of these boys cared were applying to be my potential boyfriend. I was reduced to being the lookout at the Condo's community pool.

Being teenagers it was over quickly and we were headed back, in no time.

Just as quickly, I was moving into Donnie's condo as a roommate, with Duff not far behind.

Unlike Duff and I, Donnie wasn't a beach bum. He worked long hours for a man in San Clemente who made furniture, or so he said.

I had lived with Donnie for three years and I knew little about him. None of us spoke of our home life, we didn't dwell on the past. We lived for the now and we didn't worry about the future. We assumed we had all the time in the world.

I have only heard rumors that my friend Donnie McPhedran died of AIDS.

Even in this era of Google, I am unable to confirm that he died. There is no quilt panel for him, nor have I found an obituary. I last heard he was tending bar in Palm Springs.

Although he may not have died of AIDS, I still consider Donnie McPhedran lost to AIDS.

We lost so many.

Some died by their own hand.

Some disappeared in drink and drug.

Many just shut the door and retreated into their sorrow.

To avoid the fear of catching AIDS, like an ostrich I buried my head in the sand of a volleyball court in Manhattan Beach, I hid among straight people, going to weddings and baptisms.

"It shoulda been you!" a grief-stricken mourner seethed at me at an aquaintance's funeral. "Tramp!"

Maybe, like me, Donnie simply went into hiding.

After two months with me on a cross-country road trip- there were six of us in my Camaro convertible, Donnie was the one who had to sit on the bare hump between the bucket seats, I don't blame him for ditching us.

Once we got back to Laguna, we never saw each other again.

Southern Nights | CHAPTER 17

Riccardo refused our offers of help to wash up. We soon learned in Tennessee that staff found it patronizing. We just thought he was over us. We stole one last glance at his rippling physique as he scoured the pots and we headed upstairs to our rooms.

"Will there be turndown service?" Duff flirted.

This re-infected us with the giggles. We tee-hee'd all the way to our rooms. Donnie kept shushing us. I was hoping to find family photos lining the staircase, but only found watercolors of the home. I wanted to get another look at Toby, the owner's son.

Our rooms each had a king-sized bed. They were connected by a shared bathroom. We bickered over who had to sleep with whom. There would be three of us to a bed. Duff pointed out that both Dean and I were too tall to share the same bed, there would be no room for a third. Dean, Duff and Stevie B dragged their bags through the bathroom to the opposite room. This started Donnie laughing about a Stevie B sandwich.

I got lucky, I had little Donnie and John in my bed, they wouldn't take up much room. The rooms were done in nautical décor, the beds were piled high with throw pillows embroidered with shells and anchors. Naked and ready for bed, Donnie began the arduous task of removing the pillows. With a moue of distaste, he held one out between pinched fingers as if it were limburger.

"Madame's taste is pedestrian," he declared.

This brought us to tears.

"Have you seen these pillows?" He shouted to the other room.

"Do you mean *these* pillows?" Duff said as he threw one from their bed through the bathroom.

"Don't you dare, Donnie!" as he wound up to toss it back into the other room.

My friends were having a naked pillow fight and giggling like the pink ladies in Grease, "*As for you, Troy Donahue, I know what you wanna do.*"

"Stop it, you guys!" I begged, "Riccardo will be pissed."

Luckily nothing was broken, I had to straighten the "Life's a Beach," print that hung over the bed. Perhaps Madame was also registered at the flea market. This was a hostess gift that we could afford.

"I need a glass of water," Duff calls out as he walks naked down the hall. Hoping to bump into Riccardo, no doubt.

"There are glasses in the bathroom," I thwart him.

"Where do you think he sleeps?" John asked from under the covers.

The thought of a strange man laying naked under the same roof had us giggling nervously. It was well past midnight and none of us could fall asleep. Like a yawn, our giggles were contagious. I'd hear one ricochet through our room and land in the other bedroom. There would be silence and then someone, like a fart, couldn't hold it. These giggles were like the last seconds of microwave popcorn. There'd be silence and you'd think it was finished. But then another one pops. Our giggles were like hiccups, contagious yet impossible to stop.

"Y'all shut up, we're trying to sleep over here." Stevie B whispered and threw a pillow to punctuate his request.

Buck naked, Donnie and John jumped out of bed and ran to the other room to wrestle Stevie B. Alone, I couldn't differentiate the squeaks from the bed as wrestling or sex. I considered taking the left-over Quaalude from last night so that I could fall asleep. Soon I heard giggles from the other room, my friends weren't having sex.

I awoke to the sound of seagulls and giggles. Donnie and John never came back to my bed. When I checked, nobody was in the other bedroom that morning. The giggles were coming from outside. My friend's had found the widow's walk and were spying on Riccardo. He was doing push-ups on the dock in only tighty-whities. I did 50 push-ups in my empty room and tugged on my dick. Pumped, I swaggered into the backyard. I stood above Riccardo as he finished his push-ups.

"Should we strip the bedclothes?" I asked as seductively as I could.

He stood up facing me and shook his head no. My gaydar no longer pinged. He looked straight without his linens and covered in sweat. I wanted to smell it on my skin.

"Your arms are huge!" I gushed.

"The secret is to focus on the triceps." Most body-builders can't resist expounding on the minutia of their training regimen.

I tried to wrap my hand around his bicep. He laughed. I couldn't. My hands were huge, but couldn't circle his bicep. Straight guys loved this. I had managed to collect the sweat dripping down from his pits. My friend's snickered from the widow's walk when they caught me sniffing my fingers.

"Get Down from there!" Riccardo yelled.

He had not used, "Please."

I sensed we had pushed him to his limit.

"We'll get out of your hair," I apologized, wondering if we should leave him a tip.

Upstairs, the boys had already stacked the pillows back on each bed. Stevie B had thrown an equal amount of polo shirts on the bed. He would pick one out of his packed bag, smell it and toss it on the bed.

"These stink!" he whined.

"Do they smell like this?" I ask putting my fingers under his nose, and rubbing in the fact that I touched Riccardo.

We each put on the polo shirt that we wore last, so that the stink would be ours. Stevie B left a message at the Hilton for Jim Moniz, after politely asking if he could use the telephone. Scanning the room to make sure we didn't leave anything, I spotted a framed photo of Toby standing on this dock in waders, his arm around Riccardo. His body was as beautiful as I imagined it. I was surprised he was a ginger. I was tempted to steal it and blame it on John.

Riccardo was dressed in his linens when we said our goodbyes, his dark hair was parted and oiled, his skull was square like a Cane Corso dog's. We each shook his hand and thanked him, as if in a receiving line.

We squeezed into the Camaro yet again. Both Donnie and Duff wanted to drive. Even though he didn't have a driver's license, I let Duff drive as he had the better seat to vacate. I didn't want Donnie's hump.

A half hour out of Galveston, a downpour caught us with our top down. We still had a quarter of a tank of gasoline. My fingers still smelled of Riccardo. When we stopped to put the top up, Duff let Donnie drive. Duff wanted his seat back.

"Hell no." I had never ridden in the back seat of my own car.

The summer rain beat the convertible top like a drum. I was cozy and snug with all my best friends. This was happiness. But, lordy did our shirts stink. Somehow, we made it to New Orleans without having to buy more gas. I didn't know how much money we had left. The Hilton was easy to find.

In an old city that didn't have any skyscrapers it was easy to spot the modern tower. Spoilt by Riccardo, we let the bellboy take our bags. I dabbed a little of Camille's Lauren perfume on me to cut the stink, before we went to the front desk. I needn't have bothered because New Orleans stank worse than we did. We were soaking wet, leaving puddles on the marble floor. Although this Hilton was a new hotel, it was old-fashioned and boring compared to the Hyatt in Dallas.

I preferred the concrete and burnt orange shag of the Hyatt to the marble and brass of the Hilton. Jim Moniz beckoned us to come meet the other old queens he was with. Noting our resemblance to drowned rats, He intercepted us and shuffled us into the elevator. Once again, just a week after the Go-Go's debacle, we were not the trophy twinks he wanted to show off.

On the top floor he had reserved the Presidential Suite for him and Steve. And the adjacent room for us. Their suite had a living room and a dining room. Ours had 2 queen beds and a view of the Mississippi. Stevie B was dragged through the communicating door to their suite.

"Why don't' you boys clean up and go down to the buffet, while Steve and I get reacquainted?" Jim commanded.

"We can't," we whined.

"We are out of clean clothes," Duff explained. In a grand gesture, Jim rang and requested that our clothes be cleaned for this evening. Whatever indignities Stevie B must suffer, clean polo shirts for us was worth whatever blow jobs were required.

Worried that our tans were fading, we put on bathrobes and went looking for the pool. We made a beeline for the pool bar.

"May we see your room keys?" A snotty manager stopped us to ask.

"If you must," Duff huffed, like a Gabor, rolling his eyes and pointing to Hilton embroidered on the robe.

The manager became apologetic and obsequious when he saw the room number. "Please allow me," he secured us five chaise lounges by the pool.

Duff must have taken Stevie B's key for the presidential suite.

"We'll need another," Duff snapped, then sashayed to the pool bar. "Five Strawberry Daiquiris," he flashed his key as if it were a letter of credit.

We kept her blender going the rest of the afternoon.

No longer giggling, we were laughing boisterously. Giddily recounting our sexual escapades.

"That Rodeo Clown had a Dick of Death,"

"That black cowboy fucked my feet."

"Surely, you can't be serious," Dean said having slept through that episode.

"*Don't call me Shirley*," movies informed our conversation.

"I'm as serious as cancer."

In disgust, the guests around us started to pack up and leave the pool. I was concerned we were being too flamboyant. Fueled by rum we were loose and flouncing around as if we were on West Street Beach. We were cruising every attractive man at the pool. Some of them caught us and turned red with rage.

"She was already pink from the sun," Duff pointed at the angry man.

I was too drunk to worry about consequences.

"I feel like a cat on a hot tin roof," Duff vamped.

"*Tin Roof Rusted!*"

"Jinx!"

We had never experienced heat like this. We bobbed around in the pool sipping through our straws.

"Don't you Dare!" I shrieked at Donnie, who I suspected was going to pee in the pool.

Like a Chihuahua you recognize the face they make when they are ready to do their business. Maybe he really did have a tiny bladder.

"Let's look for glory holes in the Damron Guide," I shouted across the pool.

Duff was mortified, "Way to out us, Church!"

Always concerned about appearing discreet, I would be the one to let the cat out of the bag. Duff was sashaying around the pool, pink drink in hand, like Marilyn Monroe.

"Hon, where are you going?" Dean honked.

The snotty manager presented our check, "Please visit us tomorrow," he choked on the words. We hadn't noticed we were the only guests left.

"Oh my god," Dean exclaimed, "it's $200."

"Just sign it to the room," Duff coolly instructed Dean, "and add a 25% tip."

"What's 25%?"

"For chrissakes, leave her $50."

Like a clutch of chickens we walked back to the hotel tower. Chicken is what young gay boys were called before *Grease* producer Allan Carr coined the term twink. Before entering the lobby, Duff draped his bathrobe over his shoulders like Joan Crawford. Everyone else did the same. Duff was an influencer. Determined to appear butch, I futilely dug my arms into the sleeves. Drunk, I was tangled up. It looked like I was wearing a strait jacket.

With all eyes on us, we were a murder of showgirls entering the elevator. Like a secretary, Duff licked his finger and pressed the PH button. On the ride to the top I sniffed my fingers for a reminder of Riccardo, but only smelled chlorine.

We didn't hear any giggles through the communicating door. Nobody was laughing in the Presidential Suite. The raised voices suggested a fight. Duff rang room service and joined the fight. Five Filet Mignons was an uppercut to the chin.

"With Bernaise," I requested.

More, More, More | CHAPTER 18

Like the chalk artwork on the sidewalks outside St. Louis Cathedral after a sudden rain, our days in New Orleans were colorful but a blur.

We spent the week drunk. Walls of frozen daiquiri machines spun like washing machines at a laundromat. I tried to drag my friends away. This road trip was supposed to keep us away from drinking and drugging our way through summer.

"You're not the boss of me!" Stevie B spit.

I was the most uptight teenager. I was bossy.

I wanted to see the sights, my friends wanted to be the sights.

Emboldened by the frozen daiquiris, we walked militantly through the Vieux Carre hand in hand. Drunk, we were flamboyantly, in-your-face-gay. We acted like we had invented homosexuality. We wanted to offend everyone.

We would howl, "A-Wooooo," at a cute guy. This howl was a more guttural wolf whistle. This was the mating call of the 1970's.

I was lonely traveling with couples. Everyone walked hand in hand. I had no one to hold my hand.

"Get me off this fucking Ark!" I cried.

Like boarding Noah's ark, they walked 2 by 2 up Bourbon street. I felt like a lone giraffe bringing up the rear.

We walked everywhere, according to the pictures I still have. We walked railroad tracks along the river.

We took a Paddle Wheeler up the Mississippi. The Cotton Blossom.

These are the sights that fascinated us enough to take a picture. Some lady's clip on earrings made us laugh like we were still in Galveston. (We were teenagers).

These nun's shoes. I was obsessed with different variations of the collective noun for a group. (I was in college).

Grammatically, the six of us would be a Gaggle of Gays, or an Ostentation of Peacocks. The collective for these four nuns would be an Unkindness of Nuns. Eight years in parochial school had left their mark. I was holier than thou. I was self-righteous, I was bossy. I believed sin lurked around every corner. We found it around the corner on Burgundy Street at Rawhide, a gay bar. As we slurped on daiquiris men slurped on us. Right at the bar! It was sleazy in the big easy. Men were having sex on the pool table.

We didn't play pool, we played Pac Man. Every Day. Outside the humid air was thick as molasses.

Inside the bars were air conditioned. Somehow, we always had enough quarters to play Ms. Pac Man. We didn't want for money our entire time in The Big Easy.

All I wanted was a boyfriend.

I watched the couples play video games for hours in dark bars. In dive bars, I cried as frequently as it rained.

"Tell your mama," An old gray haired black woman in a church dress pressed my head against her bosom. "What's the matter, honeychile?" she stroked my head with her gloved hands.

I poured my heart out to this kindly old woman. "I'll never find a husband," I boo-hoo'd.

She put a gloved finger to my lips to shush me. The glove was powder blue matching her hat and pocket book. She sat down very close to me. She rubbed my shoulders while I sobbed, she had strong hands.

"Be a good boy and fetch your mama a beer." She guzzled hers as fast as I did mine.

I wondered what my friends would think. They still weren't over Mr. Johnson.

"What's your name ma'am?"

"Don't worry your pretty blonde head, chile. Jus call me mama."

"What is it you want this husband of yours to do to you?" I didn't care what he does, I just wanted one.

She makes a show of fumbling with the clasp of her purse, "Fetch us two more beers, baby."

The bartender was cute in his hip hugger jeans, "Watch out for Melba," He warned me.

Melba had taken off her gloves and tucked them in her purse. Her hands were rough and calloused as she took mine and drew me in for a kiss. I was drunk. Her lips were as soft as a teenager's. I didn't care if she was as old as Stevie Bs sugar daddy. It was nice to be listened to.

Melba asked again, "What is it you want your husband to do to you?"

I could no longer ignore the sexual innuendo of the transitive verb. She forced me up against the wall like a lady cop.

"Stop it! Duff, Help!"

"Ain't nobody gonna help you when you're legally married. You gotta mind your husband and let him take what's his."

"Donnie! Help," Donnie hit her with her own purse and knocked her gray wig off.

The cute bartender made us leave. Melba stayed and watched Duff and Stevie B finish Ms Pac Man gobbling cherries on the video screen. Luckily, I still had mine.

The rest of the week was a blur of buffets.

And shopping. "You can't buy anything!" I nagged on Royal Street. "There's no room in the trunk."

"Donnie! You should have let Melba kill him!"

I tagged after my friends who wished me dead, "Guy's check out this hitching post." I marvelled at an old hitching post on Chartres street.

"Hurry Up! We had those in Bisbee."

"I'll Find you."

My friends were easy to find in their rainbow of Polo shirts. That morning they had arrived in our room, cleaned and wrapped up with a bow, like Christmas presents. Presents for Stevie B kept arriving all morning, boxes from Neiman Marcus and International Male. Jim had taken Steve shopping at Maison Blanche while we ordered Eggs Benedict from Room Service, "Extra Hollandaise, please."

Stevie B was a nice, quiet boy. He wasn't like the flashy whores on West Street Beach, flown in from Fire Island.

"Why are you selling your soul for a Polo shirt?" I begged.

Those nuns had done a number on me. He came from a loving family, we stopped and met his sister as we were leaving California. At 19 there was so much I didn't understand.

I did understand, I couldn't be owned, and I wouldn't be humiliated (at least until I got a real job in corporate America).

I was miserable about our fancy dinner at Galatoire's. I protested having to wear the gauzy white linen pants that Jim had flown in from International Male.

"Duff! I can see your bush plain as day."

"I'm not on the menu," Duff snapped at a fellow diner at the restaurant.

We were wearing sport coats. Galatoire's had a dress code. Duff buttoned his so that it covered his basket. This reminded me of the see-through pajamas Barbra Streisand wore when she accepted her Oscar.

That same fellow looked me up and down and said, "You must be Jewish."

I thought it was the most ridiculous thing I had ever heard. I was 6'3" and beach blonde, with a perfect Aquilon nose. Jim Moniz chuckled, this was the first time I had ever seen him smile. He was a proper Bostonian.

"I'll have the She Crab soup with a buttery Chardonnay, Far Niente." I ordered.

"Monsieur, I'm sorry, We only serve French wine."

So much for putting on airs. Only later in life, did I learn that She Crab soup is peasant food originally made in the low country.

"Might I suggest, the Dungeness Crab Cake with Remoulade."

"Yes, please and a glass of Dom Perignon."

The waiter exchanged a glance with Jim. I didn't understand that fine champagne was never served by the glass. The sommelier presented me with the bottle at Jim's direction. Jim and I had achieved a détente after the International Male incident.

"You're being the Big Difficult in the Big Easy," he scolded.

Proudly, I directed the sommelier to pour the table a glass. Sexy dark eyed busboys scurried about the table distributing crystal flutes. They looked like Riccardo.

I stood up and proposed a toast, "To Jim Moniz for showing us a great time in the Crescent City. And to Stevie B for showing Jim a good time in the presidential suite. Thank you, both. We will never forget this!"

I finally understood Jim Moniz was subverting the stuffy dress code. I was in on the joke. I left my coat unbuttoned. The nuns could go to hell.

When The Saints Go Marching In | CHAPTER 19

My friends weren't cursed with my Catholic upbringing. They didn't know who St. Christopher was, I had to explain why his medal hung from the mirror of the Camaro. The medal was a compromise when they removed the statue of Mary from the dash.

They didn't know which Mary was on the dash. Mary Magdalene, they were familiar with because of the hit song, *"I don't know how to love him."* The distinction between virgins and whores was of no concern to them. Having a Sugar Daddy didn't necessarily make you a whore.

They never had to suffer an Unpleasantness of Nuns. I still remember Sister Josepha Maria shaming me for holding Timmy Shuck's hand on the playground in second grade.

Fuck them. Now I am sitting with six other abominable boys in see-through trousers drinking champagne made by monks, Dom Perignon.

They can have their vows of poverty.

And chastity.

I had caught the eye of a young cowboy when the entire restaurant turned to gawk at the commotion at our table. His interest was as transparent as my harem pants.

It was our last night in New Orleans.

At the largest table at Galatoire's, Jim Moniz was making plans for after Stevie B returns to California. There were to be trips to New York, London and China.

In a rage, Stevie B stands up, drunkenly shouting at Jim, "I don't wanna go to China!" Nixon had just made travel to China possible.

Even Duff couldn't get him to sit down. Our table was in the center of the room. He continued to stand swaying. He had a glass of champagne in one hand and a crab leg in the other.

He was wagging the crab leg at Jim like a nun wielding a ruler, "I don't wanna go to China!" he repeated, "you can't make me!"

Like in a car crash, I registered three things at once, that the Maître D was headed our way, that Stevie B was uncircumcised, and that the cowboy was cruising me.

The next thing I knew we are running down Dauphine Street.

We had dropped our sport coats at the headwaiter's feet. "Why youse runnin, you in trouble or sumptin?"

A blue Continental sedan drives next to us, its whitewall tires halfway up on the sidewalk, the French Quarter Streets are narrow and the 1979 Continental is wide. In fact, this dark blue Collectors Series is to be the last of the big Lincolns before they downsized them in 1980. The driver stops the car. The man opens the back door like a barricade, blocking our way.

"Get in!" the man says brandishing a $50 bill at me like a revolver.

"Do it! It's time for you buy drinks for us." My friends pushed me inside.

I am reminded of Saint Maria Goretti who was stabbed to death for resisting rape. In grade school, the sister's explained rape as "pulling your pants down for a stranger."

I abandoned any outside chance I had of being beatified by getting into the Continental and pulling my pants down. If these goomba's knew what a car nut I was, they could have saved $50. I would do anything for a ride in a Continental. I was caressing the tufted leather while he caressed me, I was flicking the snap on the ashtray cover to pop it open while, never mind... Running my toes through the shag carpeting sent me over the edge. They dumped me on the corner of Iberville. I noticed the Jersey plates on the Continental. I was lucky to be alive. Their Continental had a statue of the Virgin Mary on the dash. I had $50 in my pocket. When a Catholic falls we really fall hard.

"Hey you!" I wasn't surprised to see the cowboy from Galatoire's standing there, but I was surprised that he didn't say "Howdy." He took my hand, and we walked up the street.

Finally, I had a boyfriend.

He was as tall as me, but much more muscular. But I was more masculine. He had a shock of curly hair.

"I'm originally from Nebraska," he lisped.

I dreamed of finally being a couple.

He pulled me close as if he were going to kiss me, "Fuck me like the pig I am," he said, Instead of whispering sweet nothings to me. His ass was even more spectacular than Duff's.

"We'll be in LA for 8 weeks beginning the 27th."

I wondered if he would use an airline pass like Mr. Johnson. I had him pegged for a Flight Attendant. I let go of his hand.

This was not the boyfriend that I dreamed of.

"Want to take a swim?" We had stopped in front of a fancy hotel. I wanted to show him off to my friends. "C'mon, it's a great way to beat the heat."

"Sure," I said, disappointed, pitching my voice deep. "But, I don't have any swim trunks." He looked like my size and I thought he would loan me a pair. Instead of walking me to his room, he walked us to the pool. He stripped down to his tightie-whities. "I don't have any underwear!"

"I noticed at the restaurant," he winked.

We were skinny dipping in the courtyard pool of a fancy hotel. The water ripples from the lighted pool shimmered against the windows of the hotel. Most of the rooms were dark. I relaxed a little thinking they were empty. He played a cowboy in the national tour of *Best Little Whorehouse*.

He was hoping to be cast in the new Dolly Parton, Burt Reynolds movie. Things were getting heated in the pool. I pulled myself out of the pool, as if we were playing Marco Polo. Hoping he'd take me to his room.

"I can't."

"Is your Sugar Daddy sleeping?" without shame, he confesses right away. "Chorus boys can't survive in Manhattan without a sugar daddy."

I get back in the pool, having lost my ardor. I start chattering nonstop. I tell him about our trip, I mention the contretemps with Melba.

"Oh My God! Mel is here?" He promises to tell me the whole story if I pork him.

I got the full story, Melba was an escaped convict who hid out as an old black mammy on Christopher Street. Mel was a hot young chorus boy falsely convicted of grand theft after he dumped his Sugar Daddy, a Broadway producer. The sugar daddy accused him of stealing a Cartier Tank watch that was given as a gift.

Half of Broadway knew it was a gift, his benefactor had proudly shown pictures of his boy with the gift. Mel wearing the Cartier Tank watch.

"It was strapped around his dick!" my chorus boy said. "Those pics were proof that he didn't steal it." The judge ruled that he would not allow such lewd photographs in his court room. None of the actors who had seen the pic would jeopardize their career to testify. Mel was sentenced to Rykers Island prison.

"I'm happy to hear Melba is back home," my chorus boy said. "Saints be praised."

Walking back to my hotel I recognize his story was the plot from *Some like it Hot*. I believed everything I was told in the 80's. Eventually I was given a Cartier watch, but I wore it on my wrist.

Last Chance Texaco | CHAPTER 20

"Don't stop 'til we get to Miami." I knew better than to argue with my friends when they were hungover. I let Stevie B drive and agreed to leave the convertible top up so that it was dark inside and we were in the shade. It was only 11:00 AM and already 100 degrees.

We made it out of New Orleans alive.

Our luck was still holding. We still had some money. We hadn't yet needed a spare tire. I often wonder if we were the last worry-free generation. We didn't have a care in the world. GPAs and careers were well into the future. We had faith that everything would work out all right.

We were dead wrong, but we didn't know it then.

Through half-open eyes we watched the Florida Panhandle whizz by at 70 MPH. There were no state troopers hiding in the kudzu. We were still pushing our luck. The speed limit was 55 (the dreaded Double Nickel). Just outside of Tallahassee, Stevie B was pushing 100.

"Slow Down!" I whined.

"I can't!" Stevie B took his foot of the accelerator.

The Camaro kept racing. Donnie reached into the footwell and pried the accelerator loose. The car slowed down. We coasted onto the shoulder. Under hood, Donnie and I determined that the return spring for the accelerator pedal had jammed at the carburetor. We nursed the Camaro along the shoulder. At the next offramp we found a service station.

"Your motor mounts are busted." The mechanic was a tall skinny redneck. He was cute with big ears like Eb on Green Acres.

"I bet he's hung like a horse," Donnie giggled.

"What's the best you can do? We don't have any credit cards and are flat broke."

I knew enough about cars that this could be expensive. You had to pull the motor to get to the motor mounts. I said my prayers to St. Christopher. We moped around the offramp, looking for a Ms Pac Man or some other way to kill time.

"I'm bored!" Dean whined.

"Let's Eat," Duff said.

"We can't. we might need the money to fix the car." I cautioned.

"I'm gonna eat!" Donnie said defiantly, marching towards the truck stop. The trusty Damron Guide claimed this Truck Stop was cruisy. (AYOR). Donnie was headed for a glory hole.

Dean, Duff and Stevie B fidgeted in the shade of a live oak dripping in Spanish Moss.

Somehow this was my fault.

John from Santa Barbara sat between us to insulate me from their frustration, he didn't care what Donnie was doing.

Eb waved me over, "My boss says he'll let me do it for $75. Do you got that much?"

My prayers had been answered. I was so choked up I couldn't say yes. I nodded my head, hoping he wouldn't see my tears.

"Give me a couple hours." I had $75 in my own pocket. I wouldn't have to bum from my angry friends. $50 of that was from the Mafia Hit Man in the backseat of the Continental.

"We'll never get to Miami today!" My friends whined.

Little did they know, I was never planning to get us to Miami today. I had made plans to spend the night in Cocoa Beach at my friend Kevin's. I fill Donnie in on the news.

"Motor Mounts for $75," He scoffs. "He's ripping you off!"

I recognized Donnie's bitter frustration.

Like a gambler pulling the lever on a slot machine, Donnie had spent the last hour sitting alone in a toilet stall, pulling on his own lever, hoping for a big payoff to come through the glory hole. We've all been there.

"It's your last chance to trust the man with the star."

Disco Inferno | CHAPTER 21

My friend Kevin Crew in Cocoa Beach was tall and blonde. We could have been brothers. Instead, we were rivals. Gay boys liked him better than me. He always had a boyfriend. He worked the night shift at Kennedy Space Center.

He invested his earnings in an apartment building on the Banana River. He was only a year older than us. I had met him when he lived with a bunch of lifeguards in a big house on the beach, near where my mother used to live in Canova Beach.

Michael Tholl's Beach House was like a gay fraternity house. There were multiple apartments attached to the main house, Kevin had one which he shared with the latest Mrs. Crew—one year it was a girl named Cindy, another a boy named Luis. A flamboyant hairdresser named Larry Lane had another. There was a party every night after the sun went down. I was anxious to introduce my friends to each other. Excited and nervous. Kevin was very closeted because of the security clearance for his NASA job, or so he claimed. Like me, a limp wrist made him nervous. We both strove to be straight-acting.

We pulled into his driveway, six giggling gays in a muscle car. Our mood had lightened as the sun went down. There was a breeze off the Atlantic across the street. I asked my friends to butch it up.

"Drop your purses, boys!" Kevin brought us a six pack of beer.

I hated beer, I couldn't fake being that butch.

The sun was setting over the Banana River. Birds sang and frogs croaked. A lone crane stood at the end of Kevin's dock. It honked like Dean. Jellyfish pooled against the riverbank like poisonous soap bubbles in a bath.

"Eeew," my friends minced, setting Kevin's teeth on edge.

"I've got to shower before work," Kevin led us into his apartment. He pointed out our sleeping bags arranged on the tile floor. At the sound of the shower my friends burst into giggles as if it were Riccardo showering naked and not my sister, Kevin. Donnie tip-toed to steal a peek. Dean was preoccupied eyeing a cockroach on the floor.

Protecting his lover, Duff took off a flip flop and attacked the cockroach. Dean screamed as if he were Janet Leigh in the *Psycho* shower. The cockroach took off flying and landed on Dean's curly head. I had forgotten Palmetto Bugs could fly. Dripping wet, Kevin cut his shower short to shut us up. I thought, we might end up going to Miami tonight after all.

"You've got to be quiet! I don't want any complaints from my tenants," Which was a polite way of saying he didn't want to be outed by a bunch of screaming queens. My friends were too consumed with lust to be offended.

I could tell Kevin was wary about leaving us alone in his apartment. I assured him we were going to go out. Cocoa Beach was a tourist town for teenagers, I knew we could find a Ms. Pac Man. My friends soon shut up about Miami. There was a gay bar called The Evening Edition, nearby. Bored with the local talent, we went skinny dipping in the Atlantic Ocean with some kids from Clemson. We had never been in an ocean so warm. The water temp must have been in the high 80's. We played grab ass in the waves... the Clemson kids left us with blue balls.

I knew a cruisy place where we could get off.

In 1981 there was still undeveloped beachfront property in Florida. This land was covered in a tangle of Florida overgrowth. I looked for the hidden beach access road, I knew from past visits. At midnight, the dirt lot was full of station wagons and pick-up trucks. Men lurked in the shadows. This was a cruisy area even the Damron Guide was unaware of. Ahead of my friends, I trudged through the sandy paths under a Sea Grape hammock. I was no longer looking for love, but the next best thing. My dream lover was a tan surfer boy. I searched for powerful shoulders and chests. The overgrowth was so thick, the moonlight only lit the well-trodden paths in patches.

The snap of a twig meant I wasn't alone. Like Helen Keller I used my hands to determine the attractiveness of my prey. The reaching hands and hungry mouths confirmed I was worthy of love (or so I thought). I kept my eyes out for the cops. But also, for my friends. We were skittish and shy around each other, not wanting our sisters to see us doing the dirty deed.

We tracked sand into our sleeping bags. We needed those sleeping bags as Kevin had left the air conditioning on. This was the first night we had been cold in a week. In a panic, I awoke from a dream, my friends had taken my Camaro to Miami, ditching me in Cocoa Beach.

Kevin was home from work at dawn and was on the phone lining up a place for us to stay. He had decided to come with us to Miami.

Lived to Tell

Maniac | CHAPTER 22

My friends were shrieking and pulling hair as they fought over who got to ride down to Miami with Kevin. He had a big old Chevrolet Monte Carlo with air conditioning. I chuckled over his discomfort. Kevin with a carload of screaming queens.

Donnie and John decided at the last minute to ride with me. The passenger door of Kevin's clapped-out Monte Carlo wouldn't open. That side of the car had recently been intimate with a guardrail on I-95 the last time Kevin drove to Miami. Duct tape held the door shut and the windshield in place. A proficiency with duct tape was part of Kevin's butch appeal.

I wasn't drunk!" Kevin defended himself. "I just fell asleep at the wheel."

This distinction didn't comfort Donnie or John. They chose to suffer me for the ride down. It was painfully obvious that Duff, Dean and Stevie B would rather die than spend another hour in a car with me.

Two hundred miles and two Olivia Newton-John cassettes later, we pulled into the Oceanfront Hilton at Galt Ocean Mile. My friends didn't realize we were not in Miami, but only Fort Lauderdale. Kevin had gotten us a free room through his friend

Mark McCleary. Mark was a big, kind, cuddly teddy bear, always smiling. He reminded me of the Pillsbury Dough Boy with a sunburn. Either Mark or his sister Candice were the managers of the Hilton. They comped us a two-bedroom suite on the top floor. Not too shabby.

We had counted our money and determined we had $100 left between the six of us. We weren't concerned. Our suite was stocked with booze and cigarettes. We survived off the complimentary fruit basket. The beach was the only thing we could afford.

The sun and surf erased our gray pallor from New Orleans. We spent the afternoon playing Kadima on the beach. Kadima is like pickleball without a net. Some boy from West Street Beach had brought it back from a visit to Rio. Now, we had brought it to South Florida.

Stevie B reported that the Damron Guide showed there was a wet underwear contest tonight at Twist in Miami. First prize was $100.

Our suite was full to bursting with friends of the McCleary's. Kevin seemed to know all the humpy Latin boys. Our guests decimated the mini-bar.

The six of us had showered and were carefully blow drying our hair.

'Carefully,' because Kevin and the McCleary siblings were drawing lines of cocaine. An errant gust of hot air could ruin an evening and a friendship, blowing the precious powder off the mirror.

Both Mark McCleary and his sister Candice were coming to Miami with us. I briefly wondered who was managing the hotel. We were a motley crew under the Porte Cochere. The six of us looked like a string of polo players in our matching shirts. The others looked like extras from the movie Scarface. When our cars were brought around, Donnie was back on the hump in my Camaro. Kevin's Monte Carlo was packed with Cubans. Mark and his sister were in a baby blue convertible Cutlass Supreme, with their backseat full of busboys from the hotel. In synchronized choreography we each swallowed a TP square, stuffed like a ravioli with MDA. We'd made a pact to take this new designer drug before we hit the road, so that we would just be coming on to it when we entered the club.

"What is MDA?"

"Mary, Don't Ask."

We were going to try our luck at Twist and would end the night at Salvation.

We were driving in the right three lanes of I-95 between Fort Lauderdale and Miami. The Camaro, Monte Carlo and Cutlass Supreme were side by side on the interstate like three little old ladies blocking a supermarket aisle. But we were doing 70. I couldn't remember what exit we were supposed to take to get to Twist.

As we passed Julia Tuttle Causeway, Mark's Cutlass took off like the Millenium Falcon. Kevin's Monte Carlo rocketed past him.

One by one, my friends were coming on to the MDA. In our cars we leap frogged each other. It turned Donnie into a little love bug, he was petting everyone in the Camaro. I punched the accelerator to catch up with the other cars. High as I was, I was mindful of the newly repaired accelerator. The lights on the road appeared in a blur like in Star Wars when Han Solo breaks warp speed.

We continued to leap-frog each other until we got to Twist.

Mark insisted we put our convertible tops up, "It looks like rain."

The six of us argued about entering the wet underwear contest.

"We have to! We need the money to get home!" I badgered, "if one of us wins, we all win."

"I'm not doing this! I'm not a whore." Stevie B protested.

"I'll get money from Jim." I laughed at the irony.

"We can't, we don't have any underwear," Dean found a loophole.

Like Galatoire's, which provided sport coats for gentlemen who didn't bring theirs, Twist provided underwear for men who weren't wearing any. The borrowed Fruit of the Looms fit everyone but me, I was too big.

"Only your waist!" Duff said.

A fat man was watching us dig out used underwear from a trash bag, he offered to loan me some boxers.

This wasn't the sexy adventure I had imagined. I had pictured it like the scene in *Flashdance* where Jennifer Beals gets soaked with a bucket of water dropped from overhead. I had imagined myself shaking my long blonde hair, like I did at West Street Beach, splashing the crowd with water as they went wild with applause.

The six of us were up on stage in used underwear standing in inflatable kiddie pools (to catch the water). Duff's eyes could have turned me to stone. I pretended we were in our white valet uniform still causing accidents on PCH. Dean stood there with his hands on his hips. Only Donnie was enjoying himself. He was making friends with the other contestants, all muscular Cubans.

"Miss Congeniality, quit flirting with the competition!"

We all wanted to shrivel up and die. We were shriveling, but we didn't die. I noticed Kevin turn away in disgust. Donnie pointed in horror at me, "Don't turn around. You've got skid marks!"

My recently borrowed boxers had skid marks on the seat. My humiliation was not quite complete. A drag queen minced across the stage and began interviewing us. For an inexplicable reason she was dressed as Cher portraying Little Bo Peep. When we said we were from California, the crowd booed.

"Kiss my ass!" Duff mooned the crowd.

They applauded enthusiastically.

"The winner will be determined by the amount of applause and will receive $100 in bar credit."

I must not have read the fine print as I thought this would give us cash for gas money. The drag queen droned on and on, fawning over the Cuban boy's muscles. He said he was from Miami to great applause.

"Liar!" little Donnie shouted. "He told me he was from Habana."

This was not going to end well.

It got worse. Instead of a bucket of water dropping sexily on my head like in *Flashdance*, soaking my entire body. Little Bo Peep/Cher daintily sprinkled water from a child's watering pail only onto my boxer shorts.

"Oh!" She pantomimed shock. "These boxers must be Bruce's!" She turns to the audience. "Bruce Brown. Ladies and gentleman, has struck again!"

All of Miami must be in on the joke. Of the six of us little Donnie has the best showing.

"I'm a grower not a shower," John from Santa Barbara explains.

Even we were excited as she begins to water the Cubans. They were packed tightly into their brand-new underwear. They had it coming and going. Duff's jaw was agog. We wanted to see what he was packing. Unlike the six of us, they were not a team.

They tried to steal each other's thunder by flexing their biceps and posing while one of them got sprinkled.

"I can assure you this water is not cold," The drag queen retrieved her spotlight. "It's not my fault he shrank." She continued her schtick.

The other Cuban didn't risk the cold water.

He wet his own underwear!

The crowd went wild as he pissed himself. Calculating the applause, he was declared the winner. The Miami audience must be into water sports.

"He Cheated!" Donnie whined. Donnie was crowned the first runner up and was given a $50 bar tab.

Kevin and the McCleary's were dragging us out of Twist before Donnie could spend his winnings.

Outside, my Jennifer Beal fantasy comes true, it is pouring rain and I am soaking wet. I do a dance to *Maniac* in my head.

At Salvation, my friends are whisked past the velvet rope and I am left dancing with myself outside in the rain.

I couldn't afford the $5.00 cover, so I retreated to my car. I was alone again naturally. I plotted revenge on my friends for ditching me. I hated all of them. I wished they were dead. If Kevin were so concerned about his security clearance, why is he taking drugs? If he is worried about being seen around fags, why is he in a gay disco?

I had no answers that night. I see answers today, There was no drug screening in 1980. There were no Mothers Against Drunk Drivers. I regret wishing my friends dead.

"Hon!" I clearly heard over the sound of raindrops pattering on the convertible top.

"Wait for me, Hon!" Dean and my California friends were chasing after Duff. He is bleeding all over my Camaro. Somehow, Dean bit off the tip of his finger. The Damron Guide doesn't have any listings for hospitals.

"I don't wanna go to a hospital." Duff is waving his gushing finger around like Stevie B's crab claw at Galatoire's.

Our Polo shirts look like a Jackson Pollock. Back at the Hilton, the arrival of blood-soaked guests in the lobby at 4:00 AM doesn't raise an eyebrow. We were blissfully ignorant of the danger around us.

Beach necessities, circa 1981. Hawaiian Tropic Tanning Oil, Vaurnet Sunglasses, and Boom Box. West Street Beach, Laguna Beach, California, 1981.

Duff Paddock and Steven Henderson, West Street Beach, Laguna Beach, California, 1980.

Bo Frieden's BF Bobby, unidentified dog, West Street Beach, Laguna Beach, California, 1980.

Duff Paddock, West Street Beach, Laguna Beach, California, 1980.

Camille Darrin and Joey Coons, Malibu Colony, California, 1980.

My 1969 Camaro Convertible leaving California, 1981.

Stevie B and Duff Paddock, Needles, California, 1981.

John from Santa Barbara, gas station 1981.

Road Trip: Me with a squeegee greeting my fans.

Dean Frey, Donnie McPhedran, Duff Paddock, John from Santa Barbara, and Stevie-B, Beaver Creek, Arizona, 1981.

Duff Paddock, Dean Frey, Beaver Creek, Arizona, 1981.

John from Santa Barbara, Dean Frey, Duff Paddock, Me, Donnie McPhedran, Grand Canyon, Arizona, 1981.

Cadillac Ranch by Antfarm, Cadillac Ranch, Amarillo, Texas, 1981.

Dean Frey initialing a '59 Caddy at Cadillac Ranch, Amarillo, Texas, 1981.

John from Santa Barbara initialing a '62 Caddy at Cadillac Ranch, Amarillo, Texas, 1981.

Rick Davis, Allan Carr, Steven Henderson at Allan Carr's Seahaven, Malibu, 1981.

Front row L-R: Joseph Genna, Thom Tadlock, Juan Cruz, Unknown. Back Row L-R: International Male model Steve, Billy Miller, Me, Michael Mare Le Restaurant, WeHo, 1986.

Michelle, Juan Cruz, Cori from Laguna, Me, Joseph Genna, Sweetzer Lanai, WeHo, 1985.

Juan Cruz, Me in Juan's Jeep CJ7, West Hollywood, 1986.

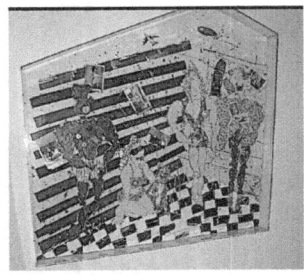

Vintage Habana Mixed Media by Allee Willis, 1988

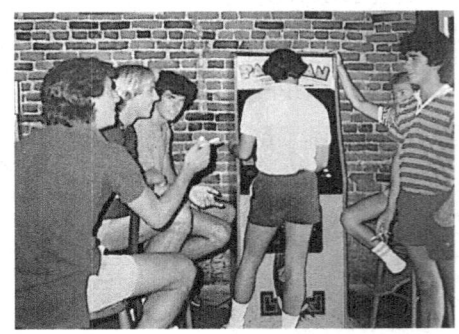

John from SB, Me, Dean Frey, Duff Paddock, Donnie McPhedran, Stevie B playing PacMan in New Orleans, Louisiana, 1981.

Me and Duff Paddock, New Orleans, Louisiana, 1981.

Duff and John from Santa Barbara, New Orleans, Louisiana, 1981.

Donnie, John, Dean and Duff aboard the paddle-wheeler Cotton Blossom, New Orleans, Louisiana, 1981.

Unidentified street dancer, Dean Frey, Bourbon Street, New Orleans, Louisiana, 1981.

Duff, Donnie, Me, and Dean hiking railroad tracks by the New Orleans Hilton, New Orleans, Louisiana, 1981.

Dean Frey, Me, Stevie B, John from Santa Barbara, Hilton Seawall, Fort Lauderdale, Florida, 1981.

John from Santa Barbara in one of our many Polo Shirts, Hilton, Fort Lauderdale, Florida, 1981.

Random hot guys, Stevie B, Duff Paddock, Dean Frey, poolside, Fort Lauderdale Hilton, Galt Ocean Mile, Fort Lauderdale, Florida, 1981.

Duff Paddock playing Kadima, Fort Lauderdale Beach, Florida, 1981.

Me, Duff Paddock and Dean Frey posing on Fort Lauderdale Beach, Florida, 1981.

Duff Paddock and his lover Dean Frey, Motel Row, I-10 East Texas, 1981.

Duff, Dean, Donnie, Me, John at a Wendy's somewhere towards the end of our road trip in 1981.

Duff Paddock flipping me off at that same Wendy's, 1981.

The dreaded transmission hump in my 1969 Camaro Convertible.

Stevie B in white Vuarnets with Duff Paddock in the backseat of my Camaro somewhere on the road, 1981.

Larry Lane, Cocoa Beach, Florida, 1979.

Larry Lane in his flea market fur, Banner Elk, North Carolina, 1991.

Martin Hoose and his lover Alvaro, Cocoa Beach, Florida, 1980.

Dean Frey and Duff Paddock, The Sheiks of Death Valley, California, 1981.

Larry Lane and me carving pumpkins in Banner Elk, North Carolina, 1991.

Reggie Feuille, Dan Downs, Le Nid Des Aigles, Escondido, California, 2001.

Porn stars under the waterfall, Le Nid Des Aigles, Escondido, 2001.

Unidentified Texas Bathing Beauties, Le Nid Des Aigles, Escondido, 2001.

Foreground: Bo Frieden in hat and tank top, Le Nid Des Aigles, Escondido, 2001.

Volleyball court Le Nid Des Aigles, Escondido 2001

Bo Frieden in his Austin-Healey, unidentified Fly Boys on motorcycles, , Key West, Florida 1960s.

Hanging On The Telephone | CHAPTER 23

I yelled, "Quit crying and make the call, Dean!" We had spent all morning on the telephone. Duff could not operate the rotary dial telephone with his bitten finger. We each had begged for money to get us back home to California.

"I swear, we will leave you here if you don't get gas money."

Dean reluctantly dialed his parents in Pacific Palisades.

"Dibs on Dean's seat." Donnie calls.

This lit a fire under Dean's ass. He begged and pleaded with his reluctant parents. Like the football jock in a high school play, he had to be fed his lines, "They make me sleep in the car," and "I haven't eaten in five days."

"I don't have any clean underwear." We prompt.

Dean loses focus, "I didn't bring underwear!"

He is cute, but he is not the sharpest tool in the shed. After 25 minutes his parents relent.

"Thanks, it's hot sleeping in the car." Dean looks confused about the next step.

The rest of us had had our money wired via Western Union. Duff decides to play Charades to give Dean his script. He mouths the word "Wired." He first pantomimes what I would guess was a string or a piece of thread. He points to Donnie who is still wired on his MDA from last night. None of us blame Dean, we wouldn't have understood that particular clue.

Fit to be tied, Donnie mouths the words, "Wire the money."

He jumps up and joins the Charade, he pantomimes a hand covering the receiver, so that he can speak without Dean's parents hearing. Frustrated, Duff yanks on the phone wire, to get Dean to guess "Wire." Landlines were hard wired to the wall in those days. Duff's tugging on the wire and Donnie's hand covering the receiver confuse Dean hopelessly.

"Just send it to the Oceanfront Hilton Fort Lauderdale."

So much for sleeping in the car. "What room number?"

In unison we shake our heads no.

"The Presidential Suite." Dean says.

We all face palm over Dean's stupidity. "Starving to death in the Presidential Suite."

Mark McCleary assures us that the hotel will forward the check immediately. He is desperate that we check out today.

Once back at Kevin's in Cocoa Beach, we are given the boot again.

"Mike Tholl wants you to visit him in Tennessee." Mike Tholl was the owner of the Beach House, the gay lifeguard's fraternity where I first met Kevin. He was a notorious chicken hawk, a man in his fifties who doted on young men. After being run out of Florida, he had just bought a farmhouse in Elizabethton, Tennessee and opened a fine dining restaurant called Park Place.

We were promised horseback rides and escargot if we visit. I knew Mike would treat us like little princes. And introduce us to the cutest boys in the Volunteer State.

Love Is A Stranger | CHAPTER 24

Once again, we were back in the Camaro. Duff and Dean continued the bickering that they began in Kevin's Monte Carlo that morning. Donnie and John were barely speaking. For some inexplicable reason, I still wanted a boyfriend.

"Why are you getting off in Daytona Beach?' Because I need to get away from your bitching. My friends didn't understand the meaning of stop and smell the roses.

"I want to drive on the sand like Richard Petty in the 1950's," I did, but I also imagined Daytona Beach was where I would find my beautiful surfer boy boyfriend. I had been hooking up with a surfer named Hal Story originally from Daytona Beach, since I first moved to California. I wanted Hal to be my boyfriend, but I think he was straight.

While my friends played Ms Pac Man, I cruised the boardwalk. My Gaydar pinged wildly when I passed a shirtless boy by the Whack-a-Mole. His must have gone off too, as we both pirouetted around and started running towards each other in slow motion like in a Love's Baby Soft perfume commercial. It was love at first site. His name was Greg Leinart. He had a lean rippling torso. His jeans couldn't cinch at his waist, because his ass was so big and firm. They just gapped enticingly as he moved. For some reason Florida boys always wore bluejeans instead of shorts. I was about to ask him why, when my friends apprehended me to drag me back to the car.

"Let's go!"

They didn't care that they were separating Romeo and Juliet. I couldn't persuade Greg to join us.

"There's no room!" my friends whined.

"He can sit on my face," I said out loud, shocking everyone.

He kissed me goodbye in broad daylight on A1A. I carried a napkin with Greg Leinart's 305 area code phone number for a dozen years, by the time I finally called it they had changed the area code to 386.

I pouted all the way through Florida and well into Georgia. I stopped at the exit to Savannah.

"Why are we stopping here?"

My friends obviously had no interest in seeing the sights of the Hostess City.

"One of you need to drive!" As far as I was concerned, they were on their own.

I handed Donnie the map and let him drive. I curled up in a corner of the backseat and stoked my heartache.

Stevie B was deep in the Damron Guide, "We could check out Backstreet in Atlanta."

"Maybe on the way home," My friends were obviously confused by a map.

Donnie did a great job driving the twisting mountain roads into Tennessee. Duff got carsick and hurled out the window. This made me smile for the first time in hours.

"Hon, are you OK?" This made me laugh.

Stop Your Sobbing | CHAPTER 25

There was a light in every room of Mike Tholl's great big farmhouse, we could see it from the end of the long dirt road as we turned in.

"Watch out, Donnie, for that chicken!"

My friends marvelled at the barnyard life darting across our path.

"Oh! A bunny rabbit!"

Their joy was contagious. I forgot I hated their guts. Like Auntie Em on the front porch, Mike beckoned us in. It was well after midnight. A goat head-butted Duff.

"Sorry about that one, he's ornery." Mike apologized. "I figured you boys might be hungry, so I whipped up a midnight supper."

We sat down at a large oval table in the kitchen. We struggled with the heavy maple captain's chairs. Duff excused himself to wash his hands.

"Hon, Where are you going?" Dean pushed back his chair to follow Duff.

Mike had the rest of us wash up at the big kitchen sink. I had never much cared for scrambled eggs until I ate Mike Tholl's.

"We just harvested the sweet white corn, The eggs are fresh from our chickens, in the morning you boys can collect more. The nutty Havarti cheese compliments the sweetness of the corn."

"That's not goat cheese?" Duff asks remembering his ornery nemesis.

"Heaven's no, it's from Denmark. I get mine at the local farmer's market. If you stay through Sunday we can go."

Mike tried to make conversation, all we could do was nod our heads, because our mouths were full.

"Now, all you boys are from Laguna Beach?"

We nod our heads yes, like six ceramic dogs on the dashboard of a taxi-cab.

"Then you must know my great, good friend Bo Frieden."

"Old Bo!" Duff exlaims spraying corn all over the table. "Of course we do! We play volleyball with him!"

Because I hadn't spoken to Duff since Daytona, I never shared this connection.

"Bo was my housemate in Key West in the 1960's, he had just left the second Mrs. Frieden. Darko, I think his name was."

We had all heard Bo mention that name on the beach.

"Has he ever got you boys drunk on Everclear?"

The mere mention sends Duff running for the bathroom to throw up.

"I see he has. Have you ever heard about the party with some fly boys from NAS Key West? Bo challenged them to a race up the old Seven Mile Bridge. Bo was in his Austin-Healey and the boys were on their motorcycles."

I had always thought Bo's stories were tall tales told by an old man.

"And," I interjected, "Bo was pulled over on Stock Island by a patrolman who was a trick all grown up!" I recited the story by heart.

"Yes, indeed. Bo got off twice either way you look at it." Mike chuckled. "You each have your pick of the bedrooms upstairs."

My friends raced upstairs leaving me to help Mike wash up.

"Did you get to see Lars?" Mike asked of our friend Larry Lane. Larry was a hairdresser in Cocoa Beach. A flaming queen, he was the housemother at Mike's old Beach House. I felt bad for not looking him up. The only bedroom left had a twin bed.

"You can sleep with Bear and I." Bear was Mike's old German Shepard. I was surprised by Mike's invitation; I wasn't his type as I already had hair on my chest. He must have been trying to boost my spirits.

The next morning my friends gathered eggs, while I fed the livestock. After our chores, Mike took us out on a pontoon boat. I was still pining for Greg Leinart in Daytona Beach. It was a beautiful day on the lake, but I could not be cajoled out of my funk. Mike let me drive the boat. He told me how much he loved living in this little hill town. He grew most of the food for his restaurant on his little farm. The chicken paillard we'd be having tonight was raised and butchered right on the farm. Mike was hosting us at Park Place. Unlike Jim Moniz, he wouldn't make us wear International Male harem pants.

"Do you see that boat house?" Mike was pointing towards the opposite shore of the lake. "I'm going to introduce you to the cutest Tar Heal you've ever seen!"

I come to find out Mrs. Widdoes son Trey is a junior at Chapel Hill on a football scholarship, and that Mike thinks he'd make perfect boyfriend for me. I was enjoying the way the day was slowly unfolding, matching the crawl of the pontoon boat. My friends were getting bored and restless.

"Lift that seat up you'll find a cooler with beer."

My friends were more interested in the boom box they found with a disco cassette. They turn it on blast and start dancing to Thelma Houston. They look like they are riding on a float in a gay pride parade, except they are on a boat on a lake in the Appalachian Mountains. Mike smiles at their uninhibited gyrating. He doesn't seem concerned about how gay we look.

"Roz Russell's made this mixtape." Mike had owned a tiny gay bar in Melbourne called Saturdays. Roz was the house entertainer. Pudgy and prone to spandex, I never understood why she took the name of the elegant Roz Russell of Auntie Mame.

"Roz moved to Atlanta and sells real estate."

Since we left on our road trip, Disco music had been replaced by New Wave on the radio.

"Can't you drive any faster?" Duff yells at me. I leave the captain's chair in a huff.

"You do it!"

The boat only had a 15 horse Evinrude. I was tempted to push Duff overboard as he took over the captain's seat.

"Hon, where are you going?"

I decided to leave him on board to suffer Dean. I popped a beer. I hated my friends more than I hated beer. The Budweiser took the edge off. Mike was guiding Duff towards a cute clapboard house floating on the lake, the windowpanes flashed with the morning sun. A woman in a striped shirtwaist was waving us to the dock. She was balancing a silver platter in her other hand. My friends were still disco dancing. I noticed a look of disgust cross her face like a cloud. She used her plump body to shield the beautiful boy who just appeared on the deck.

The boy grabs something off the silver platter and puts it in his mouth. She slaps his hand. He flashes a shit-eating grin. At 19 he is aware he can get away with anything. He's wearing a football jersey and football pants. Both cropped short. Obscenely short. The shorts ride up on his powerful thighs and bunch like a diaper. His shirt is cropped and barely covers his nipples. The top half of his football number is still visible on his shirt.

"Hey 27!" I call.

He flashes a dazzling smile.

His mother smiles a proprietary smile, "Welcome, Welcome."

Her son offers Mike his hand to steady him as we climb out of the boat. I go to reach for his hand but it is no longer there.

"You had best try these chips before Trey eats them all."

"Where are your manners, son?"

"Fetch us a pitcher of sweet tea."

"I must say, Michael, your recipe is divine." I try my very first homemade potato chip. Unlike the bagged Ruffles we've been surviving on across country, these are moist, yet crisp, and still have the consistency of a real potato. Mrs. Widdoes has sprinkled hers with barbecue powder.

"You must be Trey," I shake hands with my potential new boyfriend.

I don't feel the electric spark that I felt with Greg Leinart in Daytona Beach. My gaydar didn't ping. My handshake left a dusting of barbecue powder on Trey's hand. I almost faint when I watch him put his fingers in his mouth to lick the powder off. Donnie pushes me out of the way to meet Trey. I console myself with another fresh potato chip. I lick the powder off the same fingers that touched the ones that have just been in the Tar Heel's mouth.

I'm stuck at the table with Mike and Mrs. Widdoes while my friends regale Trey with stories from our road trip, "These Cadillacs have our initials carved into them."

Although blasé with me, their voices betray their excitement.

"I'll show you somethin' you ain't never seen before." Trey tries to one up my friends. I'm wondering if he is going to whip out his dick. Yes, I'm the only one with a beer buzz at 10:00 in the morning. "Mr. Tholl, can we take your boat to Cupid Falls?"

"Young man, you best be back in time for church!" Mike made no effort to bid goodbye to his hostess and all the boys were already on the boat. I felt obligated to be a good guest.

"You go on with the boys!" Mike shooed me away.

Trey was driving the boat. "Damn, I'm gonna miss church if this thing won't go any faster. We've got a 115 horse Merc on ours."

That was all he offered for conversation. We turned the boom box on. I was afraid my friends were going to start disco dancing.

"Put on some country." Donnie turned the radio dial searching for country music.

"104.7," Trey suggested.

His baritone tickled my balls.

"Are Y'all going to stop in Nashville?"

My friends shook their heads no. I could feel the rage building up inside me. I wanted to stop at Nashville and Memphis too.

"We should check out Nashville," I said, trying to impress Trey and gang up on my friends.

Trey ignored my blatant attempt to curry favor, and my friends just ignored me.

We hiked to the top of a waterfall. There was a line of kids at the top, boys kissing girls before they jumped off the waterfall into the lake three stories below. This scared me. My friends moved with Trey to the edge in a huddle.

"It's a piece of cake," he crowed, stripping off his cropped clothes and tossing them on a dry rock.

My friends blocked my view of his bare ass. I hate them. He was over the falls and all I could see was his shit-eating grin.

Donnie tossed his trunks and jumped over hollering. "Yee Haw!"

"Hon, wait for me!"

Duff and Dean went over in tandem with their trunks on. They were holding hands in the smoky mountains. I was too scared to jump. The boys were calling me chicken. I hiked back down in shame, bringing Trey his clothes. I was shaking uncontrollably on the boat. I had no control of my emotions. My friends relentlessly teased me the whole way back. Trey drove the boat buck naked. I was a mess for the rest of the day.

Mike took my friends horseback riding while I lay on the twin bed crying. I convinced myself we got a bad batch of MDA in Miami. I thought of Greg Leinart in Daytona and I remembered Mr.

Johnson in Dallas. I wished I could have seen Mel out of his housedress, but I remembered kissing her. I doubted jail could be any worse than the prison of my mind right now. I'll never have a boyfriend. I hated my friends. We can drive straight home for all I care. I've tried to show them the sights of America. I am not going to suggest another stop. I hoped they'd get trampled by horses.

The farmhouse was soon filled with laughter. I wanted to kill someone. I remembered the second quaalude from the bathhouse in Dallas. I took it and took a bath. My friends crowded the bathroom and got ready for dinner. They ignored me.

Mike's restaurant Park Place was a charming yellow and white wooden building. Inside two ornamental trees trimmed like a poodle's tail flanked the entry. White linen tablecloths draped the antique tables. Each place setting was mismatched antique china and silver. This was a trademark design element of Michael's, his restaurant in Melbourne Beach, Poor Richard's was famous for it. It was also famous for the beauty of its wait staff. Mike outdid himself in Tennessee.

He had bottles of Perrier-Jouet Fleur D'Champagne brought to the table. These were Larry Lane's favorite. The hand painted bottles were keepsakes, Larry's apartment at Michael's Beach House had dozens of them with tapered candles.

"To absent friends. And to new ones!" Michael toasted.

My friends twittered excitedly about the expensive champagne. I remembered Michael's delicious pâté from the Beach House, I was scarfing it down like it was peanut butter.

"That is house made pâté," Michael explained, "it's goose liver from one of the geese on my farm."

Mike took great pleasure in educating us young men. My friends clucked with disgust. Giddy with champagne, Donnie described Trey driving the boat home bare-assed. Mike's eyes widened in wonder.

"Trust me, Mike. I already licked his sweat off the seat!" My ex-friends groaned disgustedly, but Mike smiled.

He excused himself to greet regulars at another table. I dared to do something Mike had previously cautioned me against. At Poor Richard's, Mike cautioned us to never refill our own glass, that we always wait for the waiter.

"The waiter portions it so that it is shared equally between the guests at the table."

Fuck that, I emptied the bottle. I didn't care if my ex-friends went without. I grabbed for the second bottle of champagne before Mike returned. Michael busted me. As a diversion, I grabbed the empty bottle with my other hand and held both bottles to my ears.

"Do you like my earrings?" I mimicked our mutual friend in Laguna.

"Bo," the table erupted.

We had all seen old Bo slyly grab two pepper shakers at a dinner table, hold them to his ears, demurely cross his legs. And ask, "Do you like my new earrings?"

He not only did this with wine glasses, pepper shakers and cocaine vials. He once did it on West Street Beach when he was flanked by a famous bodybuilding couple, Mr. Universe Bob Paris and his "husband" Rob Jackson.

"Do you like my new earrings?" This never failed to get a laugh. I sneakily fill my glass and propose a toast to Bo Frieden.

Mike cautioned us to save room for dessert. "I made Key Lime pie."

I pictured him and Bo about our age in Key West. Now they were old men in their fifties entertaining spoiled brats.

"You really should stop in Nashville." Mike says. "I'll call Owen to put you up."

My friends were having none of it.

"And you shouldn't miss Beale Street in Memphis." He implores. "I've got a friend who manages the Heartbreak Hotel near Graceland."

"We can't," Stevie B says. "I've got to get back to catch a flight."

Apparently, Stevie B changed his mind and decided he *did* want to go to China, after all.

"My ass," Donnie says. The horseback ride compounded with riding cross country on a transmission hump had taken its toll on Donnie's butt. "I guess, you're not a power bottom after all."

My friends drove us back to California in four days. We didn't see Memphis, or the Alamo. This was the last time I saw any of them alive.

Hal Story | CHAPTER 26

Hal Story was the personification of Boy, and in my mind, he will always be one, Hal was a surfer. His body was well developed in his late teens. His eyes were as deep blue as the ocean and as unfathomable. He had a handsome, open face, with a fresh, apple-white skin tone that didn't tan although he was always outside. He had a mop of dark hair thickened with ocean saltwater, before it was a spray you could buy at a beauty salon.

He was my ultimate boyfriend fantasy.

To me, Hal was the like the first kid in the neighborhood to hit puberty, he had that confidence and that swagger. Flexing the muscles that you didn't have yet, showing off the hair just beginning to grow under his arms. The boy who ditches the neighborhood kids on their bikes to run with the guys who had cars and girls. He was always up for an extreme adventure, before extreme sports was a thing. He had No Fear, before that was a clothing line. He rode motorcycles, He surfed the dawn patrol, and he had sex.

Twice we cheated death, together.

I have no claim to Hal's memory. I was not his lover, nor his friend, we were tricks. I want to honor this boy's memory. For some reason, after countless, unforgettable men in my 65 years,

Hal remains in my memory when little else does. Over a period of 10 years, beginning in the late 1970's, our paths crossed randomly and we jumped into bed (or the bed of a pickup truck).

I want to caution my readers, this remembrance is brimming with sex, be warned there are no tender bedside goodbyes, only sweaty couplings. My only connection to Hal was sex. And sex was the reason Hal died.

Before and after I found Laguna and friends, Hal repeatedly showed up in my life—I first met Hal Story on the night before I left for college. I was cruising the Granada Beach parking lot in Long Beach, California across from the gay bar Ripples. I spotted a humpy kid in a loose t-shirt sitting on a low retaining wall separating the sand from the parking lot. I circled past in my Camaro convertible, revving the small block in the time-honored tradition of testosterone-fueled teenage boys.

Recognizing this mating call, Hal stood up, showing off how well the Shrink-To-Fit 501s clung to his muscular thighs, lifted up his T-shirt and pretended to scratch and gave me an inviting grin.

That was all I needed to whip a u-turn and pull into the parking spot, pinning him against the wall with my headlights.

"Wanna go for a ride?" I'm sure I asked.

Hal jumped over the door and into my convertible like a Duke of Hazzard. The year was 1977—the Freeway Killer was on the loose in Southern California, randomly throwing the naked bodies of boys our age on the side of the freeway after picking them up, drugging them and raping them. In fact, serial killer Randy Kraft picked up his final victim from this very parking lot.

Us horny boys were on guard, but our hormones trumped good sense. Hal said we could trick at a friend's house in Huntington Harbor. 15 minutes later we were naked in a stranger's house overlooking a boat dock.

Hal was my fantasy boyfriend, Masculine, humpy and hungry for cock. He had a big, thick football player's ass and I dove in headfirst. That's when I first noticed the pale birthmark on his butt cheek that resembled a Central American country. As I pondered what country it looked like—I sensed someone's presence in the steamy bedroom, and I felt a curious hand. I soon realized my boyfriend fantasy was an impossibility as Hal must have a lover. After an uncomfortable three-way, I took off bound for college the next day.

"We could take the speed boat to Catalina tomorrow," the older man enticed.

Like his birthmark, Hal was forever branded in my mind as a wild boy who liked fast things.

All the boys I met in college never measured up to my fantasy of Hal, either in looks or build, or masculinity. If they did, they weren't gay.

Upon returning to California, I fell in with a group of surfers in San Clemente off T Street. There was a man who had a house with a hot tub nearby—his name was Rus Calisch and he worked for Surfer Magazine—we both loved cars (he had a '71 Stingray roadster) and he had written a novel, *Paumalu, a story of modern Hawaii,* something to which I aspired.

He invited me up for a beer and hot tub and said that he had a surfer friend he wanted me to meet. I'd usually decline such offers as I imagined I had a pristine reputation to keep. Invitations to hot tub parties in the 1970's meant only one thing! For some reason I accepted.

Upon arriving I was greeted by shrill shrieks and "tsk tsks" from the naked twinkies in the hot tub, the young gay guys of my age that I ignored at West Street beach.

As these boys screamed "hey girl" and started to splash me, I noticed a bare-chested boy balancing on a plank of wood on a rolling stump, arms out like a surfer in a tube, oblivious to the shenanigans going on around him.

'This is Hal Story," my host, Rus called out, "he's the boy I wanted you to meet."

It seems everyone plays the matchmaker. I swooned at the memory of Hal. I marvelled at the changes wrought in his body since I saw him last. Out of skin-tight 501's, gaped at the waist, rose a magnificent torso, like a Mapplethorpe lily rising from a vase—and just as obscene.

In today's vernacular you would call him "yoked," but that term didn't exist in the early 1980's (nor did a swole body like his). There was no emphasis on the core in the early 1980's. The top of

Hal's buttocks jutted out of his 501s and intersected with his obliques in an intoxicating manner I had never seen up close before. I'd only seen it at a distance as I watched the tan and blonde surfers strip out of their wetsuits on Pacific Coast Highway.

Each sport develops a specific muscle group, surfers have a high curve on a bubble butt and tight corded obliques from having to clench their buttocks and tighten their core to arch their back to lift their rib cage off the board to paddle, while simultaneously keeping their pelvis pressed flat onto the board. Unlike those tan and blonde surfers who were generally lean, Hal Story was pale and brunette and generously muscled.

"Dave, go introduce yourself to Hal," my host, Russ said.

The hot tub chorus tittered, watching the "str8 acting" volleyball player of Laguna (me) cross the room to approach their current object of desire, a genuine surfer boy who was probably actually straight, rare in the androgynous world of the 1970's.

I was nervous. I was unsure if this god would remember me, and I did not want to be humiliated in front of all the kids from West Street where I ruled as king of the beach.

Rehearsing what I would say to Hal, "Remember me? We met 4 years ago and tricked in a house on Sunset Beach with a round window, you've got a birthmark on your ass shaped like Nicaragua.

I offered my extended hand to shake, Hal took my extended hand and pulled me towards him in what I anticipated would be a romantic kiss, and then spun me around to put me in a headlock without slipping off the board he was balanced on.

"Got a place to fuck?" he said to my shock, his tone indicating he remembered me, or at least, my dick. The hot tub chorus gasped. Since Hal had me in a headlock with my back pressed tight against his chest, it appeared to the crowd that I was to be the fuckee.

Since I fancied my reputation as a pitcher, not a catcher, I told him loud enough for my subjects to hear, "I can take you to my place in Dana Point and fuck the hell out of you," I paused, "again."

"OK," he said, "if you can you drive me home to Leucadia tomorrow—I don't have a car."

Leucadia was a tiny surf town about an hour south, past Camp Pendleton in what is now gentrified North County San Diego. As I looked Hal in the eyes and nodded my head yes, I caught a crestfallen look in my host Rus's eyes. It dawned on me he had been planning on driving Hal home. This is a conundrum I faced many times during my seasons on West Street Beach, "Do I go for what I want, at the expense of a friend's feelings?"

Luckily, Hal was untroubled by my dilemma, "C'mon, let's go!" he said pulling me out the door.

"Thanks, Rus," he called, obviously more concerned with who would be driving him tonight, instead of driving him home.

'Thanks, Rus," I echoed, relieved Hal did not rope me into an awkward three-way with my friend.

We resumed where we left off 4 years earlier—I had a bird's eye view of Nicaragua as I buried my face in the mountains of Hal's butt. This time, there was no third party groping their way in the dark. Hal grabbed a handful of Crisco and impaled himself on me riding as hard and as fast as if he were surfing the North Shore. There was no kissing or foreplay. I watched Hal's beautiful chest bounce and I wondered why he didn't want to kiss me.

"I'm getting close," he moaned. "Spank me."

Like King Kong I swatted Nicaragua. That brought our session to a conclusion.

To my disappointment, I discovered Hal was not a cuddler, he fell asleep quickly. When I awoke I was startled to see a stranger that I'd met before in my bed, I rarely let tricks stay the night. That explains why the sheets stuck to me. I wanted so much to know about this dream boy in my bed. I wanted a boyfriend to share my secrets and dreams with, to rule the beach like a homecoming queen and her king.

As I lay there dreaming about what a perfect partner he would make, despite the fact I knew nothing about him. I began making a list of questions for Hal: *Where did you grow up?; What do you do for work?; Do you live alone?, What's your favorite surf break?; Do you want to be my boyfriend?*

As Hal begins to stir, before I had a chance to ask my questions, Hal asked one of his own, "Do you want to do it again?"

Which should have answered all of my questions. After a quick, "wham bam, thank you ma'am," we got into my new Triumph Spitfire and headed down the coast.

"What happened to your Camaro?" Hal asked, the only concrete indication that Hal had even remembered our first meeting. After a cross-country road trip I bought a two-seater sports car so that I could never repeat that again.

"Turn off this Disco shit," hal said.

As we drove, silently, along the coast with the top down, I got most of my questions answered, Hal grew up in Daytona Beach, Florida. He currently worked at a printers in nearby Encinitas. He lives alone, behind the Liquid Blue Surf Shop in Leucadia. His favorite surf break is Swami's.

He volunteered his dream, "My dream is to surf in Hawaii before I die."

We enter Leucadia, a funky little Surf Town still stuck in the 60's, brimming with head shops and surf shops and psychedelic VW buses.

Hal shouts, "Stop," about a block before the surf shop. "Just leave me here," Hal said, as he jumped out of my Spitfire.

I wondered, then, if Hal was, in fact, a straight boy. He was acting like he didn't want to be caught getting out of another guy's dainty sports car after spending the night. I don't recall any numbers being exchanged. Driving back home alone, I wondered what to make of the night and Hal. I was obsessively determined to have a boyfriend at that time, and Hal fit the part of my dream boy. I was in denial that Hal showed no inclination toward a relationship.

I pulled off the freeway at Camp Pendleton to cruise, hoping to find a lonely marine to be what Hal couldn't be.

With the hindsight of 40 years I realize, now, that Hal Story knew who he was and was content with life as it was. Unlike me, Hal was uncomplicated. Like a teenage boy he had simple desires: Surf; Screw; Sleep.

Now, at 65 my desires have become that simple and I am finally happily independent, something Hal knew at 22. I was turning 24, and for a while I had forgotten that I had wanted Hal Story to be my surfer boyfriend, he'd been replaced in my fantasy life by a lifeguard from Huntington Beach and a cowboy from Utah.

Then one day I was scanning the latest issue of Surfer Magazine at Hobie's in Laguna and there in full color, was Hal Story in a magazine ad for *Kanvas By Katin* boardshorts.

Barechested, with those glorious muscles, Hal stood out from the other models with his pale skin, massive pecs and powerful shoulders. He was modeling a pair of satiny, red, white and blue boardshorts, something that he would never be caught dead wearing in real life. Unlike me, Hal was not a peacock strutting around—he was the strong silent type. Plus, his natural coloring was so dramatic, pale skin, black hair, blue eyes, cherry red lips and nipples, he looked best in faded navy blue. Also, the smile on his face looked artificial, it was that goofy, awkward smile, you'd often see on underwear models in the Sear's catalog. Hal never smiled like that. Despite the loud trunks and fake smile, I thought Hal was destined to be in GQ. Noticing a treasure trail of fine dark hair disappearing into his boardshorts—I realized I wanted to fuck him again right now.

Since my friend Rus Calisch worked at Surfer Magazine and was good friends with Nancy Katin, I correctly assumed he made the modeling connection for Hal. When I called him, Rus only had an address for Hal. Unlike today, most of us kids couldn't afford to have a telephone, even a landline, I drove the hour drive to Encinitas, Hal had moved one town down in this mecca for surfers.

As I searched the Thomas Guide for the location of Hal's street, which should be just past Moonlight Beach, east of the railroad tracks, I was surprised to look up and notice a printer's shop. I was even more surprised to see Hal bounding out the back door! This serendipity was the only magic we had between us.

"Hey Hal! Wanna ride?" after blinking back the setting sun trying to see who is calling him, he breaks into a huge smile and darts into traffic to get to my car. He directs me towards his apartment (he didn't recognize my car, since I am now driving a VW Thing, a true surf cruiser if there ever was one, Hal was no longer ashamed to be seen in it).

As we come to his address, he says, "It's Taco Tuesday, let's go to La Especial Norte."

Although excited by the prospect of a real date, I am wondering if the Toyota Tercel in the driveway was the reason for this quick about face. This suggestion seemed so out of place for Hal, and it aroused my suspicions.

Nevertheless, I was happy to be tucked into this dark booth in a Mexican restaurant with this dream boy who was now a model. I kicked off my flip-flop and pressed my foot against Hal's crotch. Hal grabbed my leg just as the waiter came by, and instead of pushing it away, he brought my foot underneath him so he could sit on it. I ordered the cheapest thing on the menu so that I could afford a margarita, and got happily drunk (I was only 24, so all it took was one margarita). Hal was nursing a single Dos Equis beer.

I wondered if I was getting too ahead of myself. Perhaps I wouldn't be spending the night if that Tercel belonged to a lover, or a girlfriend.

"Fuck It," I thought, "I could always sleep in my VW Thing. The seats folded flat."

"If you want to stay over, we can surf in the morning," Hal said as if reading my mind.

"Cool, do you live alone?"

It turns out Hal rented an efficiency apartment under some guy's house. Which is about all the information I got to complete the mystery of Hal Story. He did mention some rich man was building a mansion above his favorite surf spot in Leucadia.

"Some guy from Australia-used to be married to that actress."

Typical Hal, he wasn't in the slightest gay. "'That actress," was gay icon Liza Minnelli, and according to the gossip on West Street Beach, "The Boy from Oz," Peter Allen was indeed moving to California, to a property he bought in Leucadia.

We sat in silence during our meal, OK, Hal was silent while I chatted like a Patty Simcox trying to draw him out. We were out of the restaurant as quickly as if we had eaten at Taco Bell. Within minutes I was undressing this fantasy boy, devouring that amazing body as seen in magazines, touching, licking, biting everywhere-employing every secret of foreplay that I knew worked on me. Hal lay there non-plussed with my attempts at arousal and just rolled over on his belly and closed his eyes. As I mounted him and pushed harder and further, I realized no matter how deep I thrust, I will never reach his heart.

Before the sun came up, Hal woke me at dawn to go surfing. It was too cold in the darkness to get out of this bed to go out in the chilly Pacific. I may look like a surfer, but I was not.

Without coaxing me, Hal happily went out by himself.

"Don't forget your Sex Wax," I flirted.

Sex Wax was a brand of surfboard wax that kept your feet from slipping. As the door shut, I lay dreamily back in the sticky bed and fantasized of licking the saltwater off my lover's body.

Then I remembered that Hal wasn't my lover and was unexcited by my licking his body at all. Despite this realization I fell back to sleep, thanks to my hangover. Obviously, this was not the relationship I was seeking where we lay close and shared our dreams and secrets. Once again, I awoke to the new day, the back door opened directly into the bedroom. A blinding sun backlit Hal's massive frame as it filled the doorway like an avenging angel. Hoping he would climb directly into bed and let me warm his cold body with mine, a high school fantasy I still held. Hal disappointed me by jumping in a hot shower.

Freshly scrubbed and warmed, Hal was ready for sex. "C'mon, do it to me before work!"

Afterwards we got in my VW Thing. Because the top was left down all the seats were wet from the salt air. We drove 2 miles in silence. I imagined myself June Cleaver dropping Ward off at work. When I dropped Hal off at his job, I wanted to kiss him goodbye, like a twisted approximation of the Cleavers. If only their station wagon were a VW Thing, and June's pearls were my Puka shells. *"Ward, You were awfully hard on the Beaver last night."* But my dream of a relationship was inching closer to reality, Hal had my phone number and I had his address.

By the time Hal eventually used my phone number, I was actually in a relationship, just like I had always wanted, except this was with a girl.

"I can't right now," I whispered into the phone, "my girlfriend is here."

Hal said we can do it in the car he borrowed.

"Fine," Camille spit, "OK, dial a dick, I'm going home, so do whatever you want."

When I met Camille Darrin, it was no secret that I was gay, we were the Benifer of West Street Beach.

No sooner than Camille had stuffed all her bikinis in her purse and stormed off, I heard a dulcet horn honk from the street. I knew by the mellow sound of the horn that this was an expensive luxury car. Like Camille grabbing her bikinis, I rounded up some condoms and lube and hurried out the door. I found Hal standing next to the open rear door of a silver Cadillac Fleetwood '75 Limousine. I tumbled into the plush velour seats and hid the condoms and lube in the seatback pocket. Hal used a credit card to fill up with gas (I was curious to see the name on the credit card, in our mid-twenties in the mid-eighties, none of my friends had a credit card in our own name. unemployed we didn't have credit.), Hal pulled the limo onto the side of Pacific Coast Highway and jumped in the backseat with me and pulled down his pants.

Fulfilling Hal's limousine fantasy (I had already done it in a limousine, so this was old hat to me). I suspected Hal had already made the acquaintance of the rich Australian man with the new house above his surf break (Peter Allen). Unsurprisingly, Hal quickly dropped me off at my empty condo, leaving me alone to ponder my attraction to this man of little words. Boys will be boys is all I could come up with. Something Camille helped me to understand.

Boys being boys, Hal called me up two days later to invite me camping with some friends at Deep Creek, a natural, hot springs outside of San Diego. Curious to meet any friends Hal might have, I jumped in my car (I had just traded the Thing for a 20-year-old Imperial with pearlescent, powder blue leather seats, a car fit for a queen) and drove to Encinitas to pick up Hal (who had since moved out of his apartment downstairs to share the house above with his landlord).

I put on 91X a famous New Wave radio station out of Baja California, Mexico. Hal reached over and turned the radio off when Blondie's *Call Me* came on. We drove in silence to meet his friends at a Jack-in-the Box near San Diego to caravan to Deep Creek. I bristled at the introduction to these muscle-bound guys, A group I was aware of as they were the gay stars of Hillcrest. I had previously seen this group frolicking naked at Black's Beach and dancing in ecstasy (or on ecstasy) at the WCPC disco.

Already, I was disappointed in Hal's choice of friends. The biggest of the muscle boys sported a high and tight buzz cut. This

Marine Manque drove a lifted 4X4 Chevy pickup truck. Compared to their GI Joe truck, I felt like a boy driving his Nana's car.

For fun, I was able to persuade Hal to get in the backseat and take off his clothes, I pulled alongside these queen's truck so they could get a look at a real man in the backseat. An hour had passed on the drive, I imagined I could sense Hal getting restless. He had put his clothes back on and had climbed between the center armrest to get back in the front seat.

I tried to engage him in conversation, "How did you meet these guys?" But got no response.

Eventually, we were off the freeway and traversing up a winding mountain road, I was able to keep this vintage luxury car on the tail of the hopped-up pick-up, like Mannix. We pulled off at a cut off in the road. The guys got out of their truck and put their muscles to work, lugging a cooler full of beer and a boom box playing Blondie—the very same song Hal turned off on my car radio.

As I changed into my trunks beside the Imperial, Hal caught up with his friends, leaving me to wonder why he had invited me along. I watched these men struggle to pull themselves up the rocks, those gym muscles were only for show, yet Hal seemed impressed. My long arms and strong volleyball legs enabled me to quickly climb past these musclebound guys.

I was the first one in the deep bowl of hot springs worn into the side of this rocky mountain. The water was uncomfortably hot. I leaned back on the smooth bowl with my long arms spread out.

Hal was the next one up, and he dropped his jeans and climbed in next to me. Typical of Florida boys, Hal always wore blue jeans instead of shorts, no matter how hot the day. I watched Hal's friends strip down to their speedos and begin arranging the cooler and boom box on the stone outcropping as if they were decorating Barbie's Dream House.

One by one they slipped into the springs, shrieking at the hot temperature and strategically arranging themselves in this natural hot tub as they must have done hundreds of times in the whirlpool at their local Sports Connection Health Club. Soon each one of their speedos were draped around their necks like popsicle-colored statement necklaces. Not waiting to get in the pool before he stripped down, the Marine Manque took his speedo off before stepping into the springs so that everyone could admire his impressive endowment (Hal included).

Circling the bowl, like a turd in the toilet, he came to sit next to Hal. Within minutes this piece of shit was playing the same game of footsie that I had played with Hal at the Mexican restaurant. I covered my face with my hands, like a child watching a horror movie. I hid my face because I could feel the unintentional moue of distaste spreading across my face, turning me into a dead ringer for Eve Arden.

When I finally removed my hands, I caught a glimpse of Hal and the faux marine sneaking behind a pine tree beyond the hot springs. Fortunately, before I could make a scene I would live to regret, disaster struck! A surge of water, gushing down the stone mountain spilled into the bowl making a fierce whirlpool, washing most of the speedo queens out of the bowl and down the jagged face of the hill they had just climbed up. We had almost lost our lives.

In the Sunami, the cooler and boom box were washed away, which could be the reason for the blood-curdling screams. The second most muscular of the queens got into the pick-up and floored it, spraying my beloved Imperial with gravel. His face contorted with anger, eyes bulging and nostrils flared, he looked exactly like Eve Arden or Glenn Close in a jealous rage. I assumed he was Marine Manque's boyfriend.

I witnessed the whole scene from my vantage point in the becalmed bowl. When the truck hit the water gushing over the road, the driver struggled to keep it from careening off the cliff. The crunch of metal scraping the side of the hill and the screams from the queens brought Hal and the Marine Manque out from behind the pines.

As I watch this farce unfold, I was satisfied that the Marine Manque might lose his prized pick up, I was even more satisfied to see he was a shower and not a grower. MM ran to his truck and wrenched the door open to gain control of the steering wheel, inexplicably Hal was running towards the slipping truck which was now sliding uncontrollably on the moss-covered road.

I watched in horror as Hal slipped on the moss and slid under the lifted pick up. The huge tires came within inches of Hal's perfect torso. Luckily, Hal slid quickly out from under the truck as if he were shooting the tube, surfing at Swami's.

"C'mon, Hal," I ordered, "let's go."

I'd been party to enough drama for one day without having to hear the chorus rehash it. Hal was smart enough to do as he was told. He stopped to pick up a few of the full beers which were rolling down the road. Uncharacteristically for him he popped one open and chugged it before he got in my Imperial. He let himself in the backseat and stripped off his clothes.

"Fuck me," He pleaded.

The adrenaline from the near death experience aroused us both. I forgot my pique of him tricking with the faux marine. I slipped on the condom and took the proffered sloppy seconds.

Afterwards, Hal dug through a backpack and put on some waiter's clothes. I laughed, having never seen Hal in anything but jeans, but also laughed because his dinner tables won't know why he's walking funny.

To stop my laughing Hal tells me he now works at Café Europa—a fine dining restaurant in Oceanside. Which made me laugh even more, if you knew O'side in the 1980's (the clientele for "fine dining" could only consist of a couple of Colonel's wives, the few old queen's devoting their dying days to seducing Marine recruits, and perhaps, Peter Allen).

Hal tells me his landlord/now roommate works there and got him the job. He asks me if I'd mind dropping him off. I laugh to myself, lucky that I am not in a relationship with Hal, and pity the poor waiter/roommate, remembering the loads pumped into Hal.

That was not the only time Hal and I cheated death.

About a couple of months later Hal shows up in my driveway, honking the horn of a brand-new Jeep CJ5 with the doors and the roof, and his shirt, off. Despite my fantasies, Hal never took me on a typical date, like going to the movies or getting an ice cream, especially not going with me to Studio One disco so that I could show him off.

Today he wanted to take me off-roading—let me be clear this was not a date. Within minutes I was in his Jeep heading out the 405 with the wind blowing up my boardshorts, ballooning the fabric like a parachute, my junk dangling for all to see like a basket from a hot air balloon. We head out the Ortega Highway towards Lake Elsinore, through the Cleveland National Forest.

I shout at Hal over the wind noise, "How did you get this Jeep?"

Although his lips were moving and Hal was actually engaging in conversation for the first time, I couldn't hear a word he said over the roar of the wind in the open Jeep. I think I heard "insurance settlement," and "motorcycle accident," and "Daytona."

Whatever, Hal was now the proud owner of a rare Jeep Golden Eagle with a V-8 engine.

We took a hidden cut-off following a Ford Bronco, four-wheeling on a rutted mud path through the pine trees. Hal was an adept four-wheeler, a talent he no-doubt honed in the woods of Central Florida. Watching him shift the 4-on-the-floor through the gears aroused me and I wanted to fuck right then and there. (OK, I wanted to make out).

"Here, put this in gear," I said to Hal waiving the stick shift in my boardshorts, Hal popped the clutch and we were off racing across an almost deserted dry lake bed, as we rocketed beyond the other Jeepers (back then Jeeps and Broncos and Toyota FJs were the only off-road vehicles made), kicking up a cloud of dust and rocks across this vast lake bed. I stripped off my boardshorts and hung them on the outside mirror, like a pirate flag.

Hooting and hollering as we bucked across this rutted lake bed towards the other shore at 75-miles per hour, Hal going through the gears, upshifting with the Jeep's stick and pretending to downshift with mine—a look of terror crosses Hal's face. A look you never want to see from the boy holding your dick in his hand.

"Shit!" Hal shouts, his eyes bugging out, as he stomps the brakes with all his might.

My heart is lodged in my throat as I see us skid towards a precipice. In a cloud of dust, we come to a stop just yards away from a canyon which would have claimed our lives.

Together we cheated death again.

The adrenaline engorges my cock like no Viagra could. Now bare-assed in the scorching sun, Hal lifts himself up by the Jeep's rollbar and plunges down on my dick like a bungee jumper. Using his powerful arms he pulls himself up with a chin up. Soon I am using my strong legs and the Jeep's springs to trampoline him back up. Our sweat creates rivulets of mud from the dust that coats our bodies. For the first time I am grateful that Hal doesn't like to kiss.

As I notice another jeep approach us slowly, I erupt in spasms, thrilled by how close to death we just came, and by how close we are to getting caught, just now.

Struggling to put my shorts on as the jeep pulls up, I hear a familiar voice, "I thought that was you, Church—I saw you guys on the 405 and followed you out here." 'Wally Wooden was rolling down the window of the hard door on his new gray jeep CJ7. At that time Wally was the trophy boyfriend of my volleyball nemesis, Scott Nelson.

"Wally, this is Hal Story," I indicate Hal still dangling naked from the Jeep's roll bar. "We call him Wally because he looks like Wally Cleaver," I explained.

At 18, John's full lips and handsome face look exactly like Tony Dow, the actor who played Wally Cleaver.

"What are you guys doing here?" John asks, in his affected speech, still in high school he tries to sound like an adult. He enunciates and pauses frequently as a professor would when pulling on a pipe. Incredulous, Hal looks like he is going to belch in the kids face, but instead he lets out the sloppiest cream-pie fart, non-verbally answering John's question. In mock disgust, I stalk off to investigate the depth of the canyon which almost claimed our lives. I caught a glimpse of the thrill still lingering in Hal's eyes and I noticed the intrigue cross John's suburban face, so I spent some time down the canyon wall to let events play out as I suspected they would. After all, boys will be boys.

Resting in the shadows of the crevice in the cool air, I recalled how persnickety John could be, his Polo collar always popped just so, and his just washed Jeep with the roof up and the doors on and the windows up, I could not imagine him soiling himself against Hal's mud splattered body. By the sounds blowing my direction, he was soiling everything, including his reputation.

Overcome with vertigo, I steady myself to ponder how reckless Hal and I have been, almost drowning at Deep Creek, almost plummeting to our deaths here, not wearing a condom just now. It is 1983 and GRID had become AIDS and the only people talking about it were the nervous nellies chattering nonstop like Chicken Little on the gay beach in Laguna.

I had heard whispers that the model Joe McDonald had died in New York City, and supposedly a picture of me was above his toilet. That is a bad omen, bringing me too close to death. That scared the daylights out of this cool cat who must already have used eight of his lives.

Just now, standing here on this cliff was an unnecessary risk. I was adamant that I would not risk my life to give my friends some undeserved privacy. By the time I had scrambled up the cliff, Hal and John were dressed and were leaning against their respective Jeeps and chatting.

"Let's get out of here!" I yelled. I was blind with rage, unsure if I was jealous because I thought Hal and John had fucked, or if I was jealous because Hal was chatting. Maybe all they did was compare Jeeps. *Fine, Wally, you can be Thelma to Hal's Louise and fly off the cliff together next time,* I thought.

We drove up Pacific Coast Highway in silence, my long hair flagellating my face in the wind. Self-flagellation has been on my mind a lot. Am I a masochist for putting up with Hal's indifference? Or, closer to home, am I a masochist for my current living situation? As Hal gets me closer to my new apartment, my mind starts to drift to my uncomfortable living situation.

After graduating college all I've done is play beach volleyball, in the early 1980's not a stable way to make a living. After our road trip I was exiled from the condo in Dana Point. With no place to liver and with no money I accepted an offer to share a chic apartment in Laguna Beach with a Braniff flight attendant for a couple hundred dollars a month. The only catch is I had to share a bed, (platonically) with this dream boy from Dallas, when he was in town.

As always, I am consumed with lust for anything I can't have. His name was Grady Wiley, another fantasy boy if your fantasies ran darker than mine. Surreptitiously snooping through Grady's stuff I found some BDSM porn, dedicated to Grady by the author, does the muscular boy sleeping dreamlessly beside me want me to tie him up and take him? Or is he the sadist, enjoying me tossing and turning wide-awake with lust?

I decide to use Hal to bait the trap and get the answer. While Grady's body equals Hal's in magnificence, Grady's body is honed by the mirrors of a gym, Hal's by riding the mighty waves of the Pacific, in fact I've never known Hal to consult a mirror. As we get to my place behind The Cottage restaurant in Laguna Beach, I invite Hal in to shower. I'm curious as to how he will respond to my living situation, at this point it resembles his own, two men sharing a single bedroom. My plan is thwarted as my roommate is not home at the moment. Hal drops his jeans and tracks mud through the place on his way to the shower. Since my roommate is fastidious about the presentation of his apartment, I get a wet towel to scrub up the mud between the Barcelona chairs and ponder if Hal will want another session after having had 2 already today. My question was answered when Hal presented himself dripping wet with an erection, while I was on my hands and knees, scrubbing like Cinderella. My humiliation was complete when my roommate walked in.

"Ah, so!" Grady Wiley exclaims, "I always knew you'd be on your knees for a hard dick, Church."

Before, I can protest, Grady drags Hal by the hand back into the bathroom, "Let me find you a fresh towel!" he fusses.

I presumed that Grady was more concerned about water on the berber carpeting than Hal's erection. Driving home the point of how frequently I misunderstood things in my early 20's, the door to the bedroom shut with a bang and I was left alone on the floor to parse the sounds coming from my own bedroom. Nothing sounded like B&D, nor S&M, to my limited knowledge. Recalling how tight-lipped Hal could be I realized with crushing resignation that I would not be getting any of the details to fill in the puzzle of my mysterious roommate. My only satisfaction was the knowledge that a clean freak like Grady Wiley was quite possibly, at this moment, sloshing around in the bodily fluids of me and my teenage friend Wally.

The last time I saw Hal Story alive, it was fall 1986, I had already moved to Los Angeles to start a career in advertising.

Hal called me to meet him, "We can't meet at my house." he said. So, we met at a legendary surf break in San Clemente. After a long day in the office, I drove my Honda Civic station wagon to Orange County. The Imperial sold for a practical commuter car.

Watching the surfers in the waves at Trestles, I tried to pick out Hal in the line-up by the way he surfed, in my obsession I had memorized his goofy foot stance. Standing in the fall sun, it was hot in my blazer, rep tie and khaki pants. A basic Datsun pick-up truck tried to nudge me out of the way, so he could park next to me.

"Fuck off, asshole," I glared, but it turned out to be Hal, he must have sold his beloved Jeep for some reason.

Typical of this relationship with Hal Story, I never asked him a question. It was all don't ask, don't tell. It felt like we appraised each other for the very first time in ten years. Hal still looked to be the same thrill-seeking surfer boy, but I had now morphed into a typical Yuppie, climbing the ladder in corporate America. Hal took one look at the folded down seats in my Honda wagon, and took another look at me in my blue blazer and must have decided, to my relief, that a quickie in the back was not worth the effort.

Obviously, I was no longer Hal's type. At the time I sensed it was the end of something. Now, I was the neighborhood kid leaving boyhood to chase adult dreams in the big city. I was as sad as if we had met to hand over boxes of belongings after a breakup.

For hours we stood side by side in silenc watching the waves roll in perfect lines, I wondered why Hal urgently wanted to see me. We remained standing together as the sun slipped under the horizon.

"I saw it!" Hal said breaking our silence, referring to the Green Flash purported to be seen as the sun slips below the ocean.

Something I had looked for dozens of times after a day on the beach.

As sure as Labor Day signals the end of summer, I knew my Endless Summer had come to an end that day. As we turned to get into our cars, Hal flashed me the surfer "Shaka Brah" hand sign of extended pinkie and thumb.

"Hang loose," I said.

"See you," he said, the only lie I had ever known him to tell.

Years passed, fantasy boyfriends came and went, guys from West Street Beach began dying of AIDS. I read that Peter Allen died, age 48, at a San Diego hospital near his long-time home in Leucadia, CA.

Close friends died horrible deaths at hospices. The Eighties came to an end.

I heard that Grady Wiley went back to Dallas to die. My current obsession, James Stonelake was in hospital at Pacific Oaks with '"full-blown" AIDS.

I drove my Plymouth Barracuda to LAX and got on a Continental DC-10 to Honolulu, far away from disease and death, or so I thought. I hid out at my friend, Peter Lyle's apartment. He worked all night at Wave Waikiki nightclub, so I had his place to sleep.

At Dawn as he came home, I'd grab my beach towel and walk down Kalakaua to Waikiki beach and try to pick up a volleyball game at Fort DeRussy. If I couldn't pick up a game (or a military boy) I'd trek to Diamond Head to play at the Outrigger Canoe Club.

"Hey, Church," a suntanned girl called out, "I didn't know you're a member here."

Her name used to be Nina Williams (the daughter of TV's Green Hornet, Van Williams) and Camille's good friend at the time of our affair. Uncertain how she regarded me after my breakup with Camille, I decided to leave the private club before I was busted for trespassing. Not wanting to be seen scurrying away like a rat, I walked down onto the private beach and took a swim towards the public park where the sea wall begins.

Dripping wet I walked along the sea wall lusting after the surfers riding the break in front of the Ambassador Condos, an imposing Pagoda-roofed building, sort of a landmark at the foot of Diamond Head.

I noticed a man on his balcony watching the surfers as I was, the bulge in his trousers confirmed he was watching them with the same, lustful intent as I.

Within minutes I was standing on his lanai as aroused as he was. He offered me a beer. I said I wasn't sure, so he invited me to inspect his fridge. I took a Gatorade while he copped a feel. I liked it.

When the refrigerator door shut I noticed it was plastered with pictures of surfers cut from magazines, a shrine of sorts. Part of this collage was the magazine ad with Hal Story for Kanvas by Katin, right there on this stranger's fridge.

Pointing to it, I said, "I knew Hal Story at the time he posed for this ad."

The man looked at me gravely and dropped his hand from my crotch.

"Hal lived here," the man indicated his apartment, "when he was dying."

"I'm sorry," I said as I fled his apartment, dizzy with shock.

Hal was not the boyfriend to tell my secrets and dreams.

I do remember the one dream Hal told me when we first met, "To surf in Hawaii, before I die."

At Tonngs, I stopped on the seawall and gazed at the surfers, "Aloha Oe, Hal Story."

We Are Family | CHAPTER 27

Occasionally I left Laguna. I visited my mother who had retired to Florida. Having to leave West Street Beach was like being sent to detention. Melbourne Beach was only another beautiful beach, it didn't offer the earthly delights West Street did.

Bo Friedan disagreed, "My good friend, Mike Tholl has a house right on the beach. Look him up, he knows all the hottest numbers."

I soon discovered Mike Tholl's house was a gay paradise, every bit as enchanted as West Street Beach. This Beach House was a non-descript cinderblock house with a handful of attached apartments on a multi-acre lot fronting the best surfing beach on the Space Coast. This house was hidden at the end of a long drive behind a tangle of Florida overgrowth, with a patch of lawn surrounding it. The Beach House was a literal Garden of Eden where no one wore clothes.

I must have told a dozen lies to my mother to explain where I was going in a town where I knew no one. She begrudgingly handed me the keys to the rented Chevy Chevette. I had probably told her I was going to the movies.

I drove the tiny, tinny, rental car up A1A along the coast of the barrier island on a humid Florida night. At the time this stretch of coast was undeveloped, there was nothing but palmettoes and palms. Coming from California this vacant land was exotic and mysterious. Like West Street Beavh, it was impossible to find the hidden entrance. My heart was in my throat. I was certain I'd be caught in my web of lies.

I was nowhere near a movie theater and my mom did not know I was gay.

A big moon hung low in the night sky. It was too low to be of any use in Illuminating the hidden driveway that led to this Beach House.

"It's across from Holy Name Church and before The Dragon Lady restaurant. If you get to the causeway, you've gone too far."

I had memorized the directions because I didn't want to write them down. If I wrecked this Chevy Chevette, I didn't want my mom to find a slip of paper in my pocket when she came to identify the body, with proof that the deceased was a liar, and was not really going to see *The Fish That Saved Pittsburgh.*

Timidly, I drove down a deeply rutted, pitch dark drive through this tangle of Sea Grapes and Palmettoes. The moonlight was obscured by the overgrowth of Mangroves and Australian Pines. My heart was pounding, I was startled by something floating in front of my car like a shooting star. My headlights captured a burst of Lawrence Welk bubbles. These blew into my path from a Hot Tub full of teenage boys and girls in the altogether. I braked to a sudden halt to avoid a particularly well-endowed beach boy relieving himself in the middle of the drive. With his stream arcing in the moonlight, he resembled a marble cherub fountain at a pool.

I got out of my car to ask, "Is this Mike Tholl's house?" But, honestly I stepped out to get a closer look at this Greek God.

No sooner than the words had left my mouth, I was startled by a ghostly apparition.

"I'm Larry Lane," this spectre dressed in all black purred in my ear, "you must be David." He said, archly formal as he took my arm, like a determined aunt and propelled me past the antics in the hot tub, "You must meet our host, Michael."

A close approximation of his voice would be Frances Conroy as Myrtle Snow in *AHS Coven*. As we stepped into the light of the house, I took a good look at my new friend, while the rest of us boys were dressed in OPs and bright colors (those of us still dressed), Larry was dressed in loose, black Williwear, which hung on his slender frame like the Spanish Moss that hung from the trees around us. His vampire-like hands dangled from long sleeves in the humid Florida night. His limp, ash-blonde locks were cut in a severe page boy. Silver jewelry adorned his wrists and fingers.

"I love your jewelry, Larry," I complimented him.

"Don't you think this jacket needs a brooch?" he asked.

Patchouli scented his countenance. Larry was as thin as a wraith. His entire look was divine decadence.

Noticing me appraise him, he cooed, "I'm a creature of the night."

Even now, I can hear the remembered voice of Magenta or is it Columbia? Spit, "Creature of the night." In a chorus from the *Rocky Horror Picture Show*.

Pulling me closer, we enter a plain single-story house on a million-dollar piece of property, Larry Lane calls out "Michael, your guest of honor is here," his reedy voice vibrating us both.

Larry extends his hand to me, in a gesture I misinterpreted as a hand waiting to be kissed, which I did. He slaps me for my impudence and takes my free hand and pulls it towards him and drops a round white pill into my open palm with the numbers 714 debossed on it. I recognized this pill as a Quaalude. 714 was coincidentally my area code in Laguna Beach.

"We are going to be great and good friends." He says his eyes penetrating mine. He air kisses me on both my cheeks, something I had never encountered before.

As Mike Tholl approaches, Larry slowly floats out of the room, calling back, "You are the only guest properly invited."

"Not True." Mike Tholl protests, "I invited each and every one of our guests to meet David."

"Please call me Dave." I say, in my deepest, butchest, voice.

"Yeah, you invited them, alright. Through the Glory Hole at Zayres," Larry calls back, which is the only catty thing I have ever heard him say.

"Guilty, as Charged." Mike admits.

Before my more delicate readers clutch their pearls, and dust off their #MeToo hashtag, remember this all happened before the advent of Apple—there was no Grindr or Tinder or even AOL M4M chatrooms. If you were born to be an "abomination," questioning your sexuality, back then you couldn't just swipe left to meet someone, you had to walk a block from your high school and surreptitiously visit the men's room at Zayres.

In today's cancel culture you might leap to brand Mike, 44 at the time, a predator, but consider this, these "'innocent" teenagers had already lost their cherry to the cheerleader and realized that that wasn't for them, and, if all they were looking for was a place to void their bladder, the Monkey Wards was considerably closer and offered more privacy, and cleaner facilities. Having received a whispered invitation to a party through the glory hole instead of the penis they were looking for, these young guests were hell bent on getting all they could eat at Mike's boy buffet at the Beach House.

As the hot tub orgy spilled into the house, Mike, Larry and I sipped Bollinger champagne and nibbled on Mike's homemade pâté and got to know each other. Mike was an older man, a celebrated restauranteur in the area, who owned the renowned Poor Richards in Melbourne Beach.

"We are Family," by Sister Sledge was the anthem that was constantly playing on the turntable. This "'house" was made up of curious lifeguards and ambitious waiters from Poor Richard's restaurant, students from Florida Institute of Technology, the kids of the men who ran the Space Race at Kennedy Space Center and didn't fit in anywhere else, and country boys just coming to terms with their sexuality in this backwater town.

Larry Lane | CHAPTER 28

Unlike those of us who ran away to San Francisco or New York to live our truth or reinvent ourselves, Larry Lane chose to stay in his home of Cocoa, Florida and BE himself. Or, the self he invented. Larry bloomed like his beloved orchids in the swamps of central Florida. Like the flowers he was exotic, dramatic and elegant.

Watching Larry empty an ashtray or upright a stumbling guest, I realized he was the House Mother to what amounted to a cracker version of the New York Drag houses—instead *of "House of Xtravaganza,"* this was plain and simply, "The Beach House." A safe place (relatively) to explore your newly realized sexual identity, or just to cut loose in that anything goes 1970's way. Beyond his mesmerizing theatricality, Larry was kind and generous, wise beyond his years and always ready with a sympathetic ear.

Larry cut hair in a cozy beachside bungalow in old downtown Cocoa Beach, where the road splits. I remember seeing in the yard of this bungalow a lean, muscled sailor stripped to the waist bending steamed wood to form the hull of a sailboat. As the hairdresser to the local state senator Lori Wilson, Larry knew everyone, from his days as a guest at her husband Al Neuharth's Pumpkin Center. This broad circle of acquaintances made him a fascinating conversationalist. Looking at him you'd be surprised he would be invited to the sophisticated salons of the Space Coast power brokers. Of course, this being backwater central Florida, there were many places a creature like Larry would be unwelcome, like Lone Cabbage Fish Camp out on the St. John's River, popular with air-boaters and bikers.

Fortified on Quaaludes and Cocaine, Larry would take a stool at the bar, select his object of desire and lock eyes with the scowling gator-hunter and mesmerize him with his penetrating stare, and in a signature move that struck panic in the hearts of straight men with a truckload full of rifles, he would crook his vampire-like fingers and beckon them towards him. Usually, the well-muscled fly would be trapped in Larry's web. Larry had the courage to be himself.

That first night at the Beach House, Larry would rearrange himself on the antique, velvet fainting couch, not to get a clearer view of the bacchanalia, but to position himself in the most flattering light. Besides being a self-proclaimed creature of the night, Larry was a true creature of the 70's, having patterned himself from whole cloth as an exiled androgynous being from outer space. Since he would never be one of the tan beach boy beauties he was surrounded by, he leveraged his differences to his advantage. He enhanced his ghostly countenance by wearing dark colors and rich fabrics, he didn't hide his bony frame, he flaunted it, making gaunt intriguing. He verged on Goth before it was a thing. Larry was a true original in a small town that set out to crush originality. His reedy voice drew you towards him, and his sophisticated conversation kept you there.

Beyond all this theatricality, his warmth and kindness were undeniable. Plus, he was fun as hell, in that forbidden, sinful, excessive 70's way. Like, Warhol, whom he no doubt studied, kids would do outrageous things just to get his attention. Just now, as we sipped champagne, Michelle and Bobby Price were dirty dancing with Donna among the antique cluttered living room, one of them was swinging a brassiere like a lasso.

Mark J and one of the Pratt brothers, the three reigning blonde swimming beauties, were jumping naked on the trampoline of the catamaran. (Michael Kennedy had just beached this sailboat on the dunes with a dozen new guests). Their beautiful white Speedo butts were full moons gleaming in the starlight.

Kevin Crew had retreated to the calm of his apartment on the property with the latest "Mrs. Crew," a boy named Louis who had replaced a girl named Cindy. Kevin grew up nearby and worked at the Space Center so he kept a discreet, conservative profile and usually vanished when the shenanigans began.

Larry expounds on the provenance of the antique Cutler roll top desk across from us. Del is leaning into it gripping the built in letter dividers while buggered by an FIT flight instructor.

Larry's voiceover about the quality of construction allows me to gaze at the forbidden tableau and imagine that the muscular, student from FIT currently railing Dell could be my future boyfriend.

Like a maiden aunt from another planet, Larry rises and walks towards the antique, his bony finger raised as if he's going to give a white glove test for dust. I glance at Mike—his house is immaculate, despite the damage testosterone-fueled beach boys can do.

Dramatically, with his raised finger, Larry promptly rolls the desktop down over Del's head. 'That's better," he murmurs to us, as it muffles Del's Jeff Stryker moans.

I get the impression that Larry is sweet on Del, it's hard to tell as Larry is surprisingly discreet about his own love life. My fingers begin to tingle and I melt into the horsehair wing chair, realizing I'm coming on to the Quaalude. I set my champagne on the marble topped antique side table and begin to worry that I'll pass out and be stuffed into that roll top desk in this den of sin. How will I ever be able to drive the Chevette home, I worry.

The Rorer 714 works its magic and all my cares vanish. Mike senses my dilemma and takes hold of my hand and reassures me that there is an extra guest room that I am more than welcome to.

"Hullo, you must be the fabulous David Churchill, pleasure to meet you, I'm Scott Elliott." Says the charming beach boy with the unforgettable appendage as seen in the driveway. He comes toward me with an outstretched hand, and I wonder if I am to shake it or if he will drop another magic party favor into my hand. His arm quickly changes direction and grabs the bottle of Bolly out of the sweating ice bucket nearby.

"Please, help yourself," Larry says, bitingly, "you know where the crystal flutes are, dear."

Larry's tone conveys there is a tense history here.

As the Quaalude strengthens its grip on me, I marvel at the dynamics at play in this home for wayward boys, and I almost reach out to unzip Scott. Hastily, he has taken off to the kitchen as Larry rolls his eyes for Mike. Larry sinks back onto the fainting couch like a falling leaf in Autumn. He no sooner settles in than he is back up in a flash. The FIT stud has pulled out of Del in the roll top desk and has wiped himself with an antimacassar from the davenport, and discarded it on the floor. In one quick feline movement, Larry has scooped it up and tossed it in the wastebasket, while rolling up the desk to release Del.

"Don't worry, Michael, I'll pluck it out later and launder it."

I begin to see that Michael and Larry have a symbiotic arrangement where Mike gives Larry the wherewithal to entertain on a grand and gaudy scale, and Larry maintains the house and keeps the mayhem from getting out of hand.

As my eyes drop to half mast, Mike nudges me and says, "Go play with Billy Shoup," pointing to a naked, muscled urchin scowling on a kitchen chair, with a skateboard propped against his knee, an open copy of *Guns & Ammo* camouflaging his boner. I consider doing as told until two girls skip into the living room from the hot tub, sopping wet with bubbles serving as pasties and a thong. I notice Billy Shoup's eyes look up from *Guns & Ammo* and follow the girls until they jump into the orgy on the catamaran.

Mark J and one of the Pratt boys had long ceased jumping on the catamaran and Bobby Price and the girls had quit dancing and the Catamaran had become a tangle of bronzed limbs and parted lips, a Florida version of a Calvin Klein Obsession ad.

Larry gets back up and immediately begins wiping the girl's wet footprints from the terrazzo floor. I also get up to investigate the orgy and crumple to the floor on Jello legs, before Mike can lend a hand, Larry is beside me helping me up.

"Oh!" Larry exclaims. "I do wish Martin and Alvaro could have come tonight.'"

Larry has a gift for making you feel like the most important person in the room. He can simultaneously make you feel like you've arrived too late and just missed all the excitement. Like a publicist, Larry has breathlessly described Marty and Alvaro as the most glamourous couple since Liz & Dick.

"Alvaro stopped by earlier with their regrets," Mike Tholl says to Larry Lane, exchanging a significant look. "But, he did leave you a hostess gift."

Larry's eyes flash with excitement, underneath the marble topped claw foot table next to me, Mike gives Larry a hand off. Like a sneaky dad, overruling mom's instructions, Mike says, "Have Lars show you his lair."

Larry takes me by the hand and slinks off to his apartment on the grounds, like Kevin's. All eyes are on us as we exit the party.

Lar's Lair is as different from Mike's home as it can be. It's like walking into a Moroccan tent or an Opium den. Colorful, lush batik fabrics drape the walls and are strewn over dozens of overstuffed pillows on the floor, a hammered brass tray is balanced precariously amid the pillows to serve as a cocktail table. A massive four-poster bed dominates the space and it is tented with billowing mosquito netting. I puddle onto the pillows and watch Larry light scented candles on every surface, I have a premonition of the place going up in flames, as I notice billowing fabrics meet flickering candles.

Larry says, "Alvaro left me a treat, do you want some? Larry pulls out an amber vial and takes a silver spoon from around his neck and takes a sniff, offering me some cocaine. "It's Pink Peruvian just off the block," Larry points out, always the connoisseur.

Within seconds my face is as numb as my legs. As I worriedly wonder what will transpire between me and the Man who fell to Earth, there is a scratch at the door like a cat.

"Are you decent?" a girl's voice calls from beyond the door. I hear a cascading chorus of giggles. Just then I notice cats scrambling from all the nooks and corners in the room, jumping over the candles and onto the bed. I am awfully allergic to cats and make my exit as naked boys and girls from the catamaran push into Larry's lair.

"Thanks, Larry," I call out.

I seek out my host, Mike, to explain my bad manners and inform him of my cat allergy.

"You look like you're feeling better," Mike says as I steadily make my way towards him.

I realize Mike has not moved throughout the entire party, he is still sitting in the same antique chair.

"Can I get you anything?" I ask, taking over in Larry's absentia.

"Get yourself laid!" he says matter-of-factly to me.

I walk confidently toward the catamaran in search of Mark J. Although I want to ravish his beautiful body and pull his blonde hair, all I really want to do now is hold his hand and gaze into his eyes and hear his secrets. Even high as a kite I realize that talking is frowned on at an orgy.

Afternoon Delight | CHAPTER 29

"*Rubbin' sticks and stones together make the sparks ignite,
And the thought of lovin' you is getting so exciting,*"
Skyrockets in flight
Afternoon Delight

Remembering this song by Starland Vocal Band from 1976 reminds me why I did not have the skillset to navigate an orgy at age 18. Unlike the instructional lyrics of today's *Wet Ass Pussy* by Cardi B and Megan Thee Stallion, we had this and Captain & Tennille's *Do That To Me One More Time*.

"Do What?" I wanted to scream, so unsophisticated and uninformed was I back then. All I knew that I wanted to do back then was kiss M J and hold his hand and take a walk on the beach together.

Now, all I had to do was find him amid the tangle of tan arms and legs of the beautiful boys and girls writhing on the catamaran under a shining moon. I bravely tugged off my Hang Ten shirt and headed towards the petting zoo (my friends still alive who remember that day insist that I am mistaken, it wasn't an orgy, just friends laying around in the moonlight on a boat). Bare-chested but still wearing Quiksilver boardshorts, I was still a timid mother's boy, despite the quaalude and cocaine buzz.

Immersed in the sensuality of it all, it was apparent by the swelling in my boardies that I was a man, no longer a boy. As I edged closer to the beached catamaran, desperately trying to find MJ amid the Heavy Petting Zoo, I marvelled at the variety of colors of the girl's nipples, some were nut brown and others were dusty pink, and some were as transparent as the ghost crabs scuttling out of their holes under the catamaran. I was not surprised by the variety of penises—having been around Laguna Beach parties—I was impressed by the size of some of these white boys. Looking back I realize that the gang at the Beach House didn't include any kids of color (see how my mind works?), this was the deep South in the late 70's.

You kids today don't know the stunning beauty of a full bush, we had surfed out blondes with a dark chestnut bush against pale white skin, we had natural golden blondes with golden pubes, we had a few gingers, glowing bright orange in the moonlight.

I was unable to find MJ, time was running out as hands reached out to pull me in, one had even managed to release the Velcro fly on my boardshorts. (Beach boys could do what desert cowboys couldn't). I felt a warm wet mouth engulf me—even I understood it was poor etiquette to swat someone away in this free for all. Don't they understand, I'm here looking for True Love.

Frustrated I called out, "Mark," as casually as I could. I did not want to sound like a mom on a front porch as the streetlights came on. I notice a blonde head pull back from the girl he is kissing to see what idiot is calling his name. I also register the death daggers said girl's eyes are shooting my way. Surprisingly, MJ stands up shakily on the cat's trampoline amid the writhing bodies, oblivious to the brown-haired boy orally attached to his crotch.

"What?" he gruffly asks.

My unformed plan was to disentangle him from the mass of groping hands and open mouths so that I could have him all to myself, to hold his hand and gaze into his eyes and extract his secrets. And make him fall in love with me. My plan was to get him out to my rented Chevy Chevette and make out on the reclining bucket seats.

"Come Here," I confidently demand—my year as reigning king of the beach in Laguna had given me a newfound confidence, I had yet to encounter anyone to decline my invitation, until now. The intransigent MJ must not have found me his type. Regardless, he is still standing up awaiting my command.

I come up with a new plan on the spot, "I've got the munchies, let's go to the Circle K."

I concocted this ruse to get him in the Chevette and have a make out session safely behind locked doors, just the two of us. Was anyone so selfish and self-absorbed as I was? MJ obviously wasn't.

"Sure," he says, "anybody want anything from Circle K?" he calls out, and surprisingly they did. I had not calculated that the armoa of marijauan meant these stoned teens had the munchies.. MJ begins taking orders from the stoned kids in the Petting Zoo, like a harried Waffle House waitress. Clutching a handful of dollars and assorted coins, MJ is bent over looking for something, which put his beautiful white butt in my line of sight, like a personal invitation.

"I can't find my pants!" he cries in despair.

"That's OK," I leer, because in my mind we are going no further than to my parked car, no pants will make my conquest a lot easier.

Like a lamb to the slaughter, MJ follows me to my car which was still abandoned outside the hot tub, keys in the ignition where I left them when Larry Lane first spirited me away.

"Do you guys want anything from Circle K?" MJ calls out to the two girls still marinating in the hot tub—which foils my plan as I did not envision spectators watching us from the hot tub. So, I will have to move the Chevette. I drive the car a short ways down the drive into the pitch dark, parking next to Billy Shoup's lifted Bronco with the winch, and then I make my move.

"Uh." MJ protests, as I put my arm around him to pull him close.

"I thought we were going to Circle K?" He says firmly.

His hands are folded demurely in his lap covering his nakedness. My 18-year-old erector set of hormones is enraged with his rejection.

"Fine, we'll go to the store!" I bark. *If that's what you want, you little twit, I'll drive your naked ass to the Circle K, I hope we fucking die*, I think to myself.

I negotiate the rutted drive with much less trepidation than earlier, quaaludes were marvelous to quell anxiety. As I pull out into traffic on A1A on a busy Sunday night, I recognize through a fog that I shouldn't be driving. *If we die, it's your fault, MJ, you had to be Mr. Nice Guy and take the orders and you had to go to the store,* I stew to myself.

I feel like I'm doing an excellent job of driving this rented Chevy Chevette, so as we approach the Circle K I take one hand off the wheel and put it on MJ's naked thigh.

"You're passing the driveway," MJ points out.

Startled I cut the wheel too sharply and we miss the drive and end up nose first in a swampy ditch, next to a culvert. I shift the Chevette into reverse to back out. The wheels just spin. With the car's nose in the ditch the rear wheels are up in the air as I had wished MJ's legs would have been by now. I shift into park and look at MJ who returns a snarky smirk my direction, I'm sure he's thinking, *you deserve this, you pervert*. Neither of us are hurt. No flashing lights from a patrol car are in sight. MJ's Mona Lisa smile hides what he's thinking. This minor near catastrophe is merely an inconvenience, not as treacherous as trying to hide the truth about our sexuality .

This ditched car is nothing we can't handle. Then, all of a sudden, the enormity of our disaster dawns on both of us simultaneously, now our parents will find out our secret! If only MJ were a naked girl, this would be written off under General Horseplay, my mom would be happy to say, "boys will be boys," I find out recently that MJ's thoughts were along the same lines.

"What will my parents do when this story dominates cocktail chatter at the Yacht Club? He was naked with another boy in a Chevy Chevette," being found in an economy car would be the scandal at the club-If it were an Eldorado all would be kosher. I open the door to step out and my long legs can't find the ground. I pull myself up by the doorframe and lower myself into the swampy ditch. I am startled by a flashlight in my face.

A county sheriff is standing right next to me, "Looks like you're in a heap o' trouble, boy." My memory insists these are his exact words. Almost 50-years later I recall this was the punch line to a 1970 Dodge Challenger commercial. Regardless, I still believe this is exactly what he said!

The adrenaline coursing through my almost naked body sobered me up real quick! I've got a naked passenger in my car. The sheriff circles my car shining his flashlight at each wheel not touching the ground.

"What you gonna do about this son?" he asks, shining the flashlight in my eyes. Then he begins shining his flashlight through the windows inspecting the interior, my heart sinks realizing he will soon discover my bare-naked passenger. Trying to buy time, I ask the Sheriff.

"Can you call triple AAA for us?"

What kind of idiot uses the plural to give away my naked passenger? Just before the flashlight's beam hits MJ the Sheriff redirects it pointing it towards a payphone against the Circle K in answer to my question about calling Triple A. Sweat is pouring down my face and mosquitos are feasting on me as I had planned to feast on MJ. Luckily, I was carrying some of the loose change MJ had collected at the Petting Zoo for someone's Bugles order.

I tell the Sheriff, "I'll be right back."

I begin to trudge to the pay phone. As I cross the spillway under the driveway that I missed I wonder why this cop is just letting me walk away from the scene of the crime to a pay phone. If I were not such a momma's boy I could run for my life and live as a fugitive. I hang up on AAA when I see the cop approach the passenger door soon to shine the flashlight on the bare-assed MJ.

I run back to the car, "Excuse me, Sheriff," I slie, "there was no answer."

The Sheriff redirects his flashlight to shine in my face. I begin to worry that my pupils are betraying my substance abuse by not properly dilating. I mentally practice walking a straight line while touching my fingers to my nose.

"What's your plan, now, son?"

An image of Billy Shoup's massive Bronco with its stump-pulling winch flashes in my mind. Without considering the consequences, I ask the cop if he'd drive me back to the house so I can get a friend to pull me out with his truck.

"It's real close, just across from Holy Name church."

"Get in my Patroller," he orders, all business-like. "Front or back, Sir?" I ask.

"If you're a criminal you ride in back behind the cage."

I get in front—I'm not going to confess to any crime. The Sheriff opens the driver's door to his boxy Crown Vic patrol car. Just as I realize I've diverted him from discovering my naked passenger another patrol car pulls up and the Sheriff returns to the crime scene. For some reason sitting bare-chested in a patrol car is giving me an erection, thinking about handcuffs.

The Sheriff is back in his car and starts it up muttering under his breath about the incompetence of the local constabulary as we wait to make a left turn against an unending line of traffic. The sheriff raises a powerful arm and flicks the switch that turns on the lights and siren, stopping traffic so that we can pull out. He flashes me a shit-eating grin and I forget all about the movie *Deliverance* and I remember a Falcon porn movie called *Hot Cop*. I unclench my knocking knees and seductively spread my teenage legs wide. So much for saving myself for True Love. Regardless, I'd be saving myself in one way or another.

I notice my Sheriff is so distracted that he has only switched the siren off, but not the gumball lights on the roof. As the flashing red and blue lights illuminate the Australian Pines that camouflage the house from the driveway I suddenly realize the enormity of my stupidity, leading a law enforcement officer to the site of a drug-fueled underage teenage orgy.

"Stop here," I shout as we approach Billy Shoup's '79 Bronco with the winch. "There's the truck that will pull me out." I explain. I jump out of the patrol car just as the two naked girls jump out of the hot tub.

"Find Billy Shoup!" I call out to the girls. The '79 Bronco was the last of the really big Broncos before Ford downsized the F150 in 1980. The Sheriff drives further down the drive to the turnaround at the end, leaving me alone and mortified at my stupidity. Noticing my shriveling erection, I begin to feel sorry for myself. *Alone again, naturally.*

Billy Shoup uses the winch to pull the Chevy Chevette out of the ditch. There was a long standoff with MJ who, understandably refuses Billy's order to get out of the car. Year's later I learn that Michelle and Donna have christened this night Black Sunday. MJ and I had successfully kept our secret from our parents for a little while longer. I don't know why the Sheriff didn't arrest all of us.

Chevy Discontinued the Chevette replacing it with the front wheel drive Citation. Mike Tholl sold the beach house and moved to North Carolina. I don't think it was my fault.

Autumn Changes | CHAPTER 30

I persuaded yet another friend to get in a car with me. This time it was Larry Lane and the year was 1991.

By this time Larry had moved back into his mother's house, "To take care of her after my dad passed."

It was a typical Florida cinderblock house on the wrong side of the tracks in Cocoa. Cocoa itself is literally on the wrong side of the tracks, being miles across the causeway from Cocoa Beach and Larry's old life. By then, I too was living in Florida, in Kevin Crew's Boathouse, having buried my last friend in California and run away to a place that held no ghosts for me.

I had heard that Larry had "It."

This reunion was strained given the reduced circumstance we were both in. Since Larry didn't drive, I was invited to his mother's house. Mothers made me extremely nervous back then. Larry welcomed me into his mother's home and we embraced, I recoiled having felt the unmistakable jab of an embedded port in Larry's bony chest. Larry always seemed to know what I was thinking.

"Do you like my new Brooch?" he asked opening his robe. "It's for the Interferon." Doctors prescribed Interferon when there was nothing else to do to fight AIDS. It rarely worked.

I could hear his mother washing up in the kitchen. As he did when we first met, Larry took me by the arm and propelled me outside to the carport, which I interpreted as a move to get some privacy so that he could unburden himself of his diagnosis. Since Larry's entire androgynous rocker look hinged on frail, bony and ghostly, he didn't appear much different to me. As usual, with anticipating Larry, I was wrong.

"This is what I wanted you to see." Larry pointed me to a marvelously decaying 1986 Oldsmobile Ninety-Eight Regency covered in black mold under the carport.

"This is now mine!" He crowed. And cackled. "This is what my bloody father left me in his will. His faggot son who refuses to drive."

My sickeningly upbeat disposition located a silver lining, "It's the perfect road trip car!" I exclaimed, eyeing the burgundy button-tufted loose pillow velour interior.

Drolly, with a glint of evil in his eyes, Larry said, "Perfect, drive me up to see Mike." Mike had sold the Beach House and hightailed it to Banner Elk, North Carolina, under a cloud of scandal.

A Radisson Resort now presides where our youthful home for wayward boys once stood.

"OK, call him and tell him we're coming!" I still believed a road trip would solve any problem. "I'll get this Olds detailed and check the mechanicals and top up the fluids."

In the unrelenting Florida heat, Larry looks dizzy and unwell, he excuses himself and goes back into the air conditioning in his mother's dreary Eisenhower era home.

My heart breaks for Larry who always took great pleasure in beauty and fine design. I'm determined to bring out the beauty in his Ninety-Eight Regency for our road trip. I check the oil, full and not too dirty, the tires look like they're in good shape, plenty of brake fluid and the radiator is full and the hoses and belts look solid. All I need do is make a trip to Pep Boys to buy some wax and ArmorAll. And some Bleche-White for the whitewall tires. So immersed in my to-do list, I neglect to consider if Larry is well enough to make the trip.

In my excitement I say, "See you Tomorrow!" as I rush out the door to head to the auto parts store. Was anyone so young and self-involved to say, "See you tomorrow," to a man so obviously dying?

I pressure washed the mold from the paint. I added freon to the air conditioner, and we topped up the tank with petrol, for some reason Larry brings out the Brit in me.

I was never able to breach unpleasant topics, but I mustered the nerve to inquire if Larry's doctor would approve of this trip.

"Poppycock," he replied.

"Poppycock," I repeat, "always thinking of cock."

Which was not true with Larry, I suspect he was a pitcher rather than a catcher, as we said in those days. But, more to the point, Larry's focus was always the heart and not the genitals.

"Poppycock. I just rescheduled my infusion. We set off tomorrow." Larry said.

Surprisingly Tomorrow did come for both of us. We set off for North Carolina in an old Oldsmobile. As I did a decade ago, I merged again onto I-95. I nudged this long slumbering beast up to speed, watching the exhaust for tell-tale smoke.

"Stop!" Larry screeches. He frantically points to a Flea Market at the first exit. "I must shop for some new threads."

Between the two of us we only have $200 to get there and back. I caution Larry to be frugal. But I am grateful that Larry wants to stop and see the sights. I check under the hood of this awakened beast to see how she is doing, while she (Larry) swans into the flea market like Jackie O with Ari's money. Soon I am surrounded by a baker's dozen of Florida boys inquiring about the car. Surprising how many of these redneck boys took their dates to prom in a car like this.

Larry spots me surrounded by shirtless hunks and cuts his shopping spree short.

"Can I sit inside?" a cute crew cut blonde asks.

"Yes, you may," I watch him jump shirtless in the backseat and plump the loose cushion velour like a proud owner.

Looking a perspiring ghost Larry approaches us defiantly, "Picking up Hitch-hikers already, David?"

At the sight of the infamous Cocoa Queer, all the boys flee and the crew cut blonde panics, trapped in the backseat in a two-door car. He pushes every button in the backseat, turning the reading light on and off. This poor boy probably grew up in a minivan with power sliding doors. To get out of a two door coupe, one must find the seatback release lever at the base of the front seat, fold it forward and climb over.

Larry cackles at his distress and begins to model his purchases, he's bought a black ankle length fur coat, "What becomes a legend, most?" I teased him, with the famous Blakglama tagline.

"And I got this fabulous new brooch," he raises a cubic zirconium beetle and pins it to his new fur. I could hear the Marine whimper as he escapes. Like an albino Iman, Larry shrugs out of his new fur and tosses it into the mammoth trunk and slams the lid in one fluid motion. Shopping seems to have improved Larry's health, and he tucks himself into the just vacated backseat that still smells like virgin military boy.

"What branch of service, does it smell like?' I inquire of Larry.

"Hmmm, Navy," he swoons. "It's rarer than Shalimar." Larry sinks contentedly into the swaddling velour and I drive off. For two hours we happily talk about nothing. When we approach the exit for Yulee, Larry urgently pleads, "Please stop, I don't feel well."

I pull into a service station that sells Pecans and Seashells, *Best Prices at This Exit!* Tourists scatter as Larry hurriedly pushes his way inside. I've seen this before, churchgoers scattering at the sight of a queer man. Or are they horrified for another reason?

Am I just blind to how visibly ill Larry really is?

In my distress I top up the gas to keep myself from screaming. I see Larry scurry through the crowd at the door, mopping his face with a tissue.

Reading my face and knowing my thoughts like he always did, Larry says, "It was those darn, boiled peanuts at the Flea Market." Larry decides to sit up front. "This window rolls down unlike those damn opera windows in back."

Larry pushes the power window switch with his long, vampire fingers. Nothing happens.

"I guess it doesn't, must be broke," he chuckles wryly.

I question the folly of Driving Miss Daisy through the Deep South in this rattletrap of a car.

Again, sensing my thoughts, Larry says "Isn't this grand? I feel renewed," he takes a ragged breath and continues, "I'm dying to see Michael."

"Larry please, your choice of words," I beg.

Larry reaches into his waistband and pulls out an 8-track cartridge and pushes it into the radio. "We are Family," by Sister

Sledge comes blaring out of the speakers. Larry takes my hand across the fold down center armrest and squeezes it tight. "We are Family," he says like a benediction and closes his eyes. I sense he is imagining the presence of all the Beach House boys riding in this car with us, "now and at the hour of our death amen."

He is so still and peaceful, I'm afraid that he has passed.

"Larry," I scream and his eyes pop open, "did you pinch that tape?" I recover.

Hours later, in the hills of North Georgia, which has forever haunted me since that scene in *Deliverance*, we pull this 15-year-old Oldsmobile over and I use the bathroom to take a leak. I am surprised by how cold the air has turned just hours out of Florida. I'm in line to buy a Pepsi and I look out through the doors at a group of hillbilly boys fueling a pick-up truck with a gun rack, all glaring menacingly at Larry who sits in the backseat peering out the opera window, clutching his fur around his neck like a soignee model in an Oldsmobile brochure. I worry that Larry will seductively crook his finger at one of these boys, I am not up for a fist fight.

I stomp towards them as confidently as one can while wearing pink OP shorts and flip flops. Menacingly I swing the wide driver's door open like a flipper in a pinball game, sending them scattering in their steel toed boots. I fire up the 455 Rocket V8 and pull back onto the highway, we've been off the interstate for some time now. We are on a two-lane state road, winding through the hills. Fall has come to the north Georgia mountains and colored leaves are falling from the trees and fluttering in front of our Oldsmobile.

"Stop," Larry startles. Again, I assume he's going to be sick. "Please let me out."

I run around and open the passenger door, slide the chrome release lever and fold the seatback down so that Larry can climb over the seat and get out.

Luckily, he doesn't appear distressed or about to be sick.

Larry is grinning like a fool. He is standing in the middle of the highway with his arms outstretched like a child trying to catch a snowflake. I worry that this could be AIDS dementia.

Larry is running around happily trying to catch a falling leaf.

"It's good luck if you catch a leaf before it hits the ground," Larry proclaims as he catches one.

"Make a wish," he says.

I figure we can use all the luck we can get. I join him and we spend five minutes running in circles catching leaves until we fall down, dizzy, on the highway, tears of laughter in our eyes.

I hope Larry sensed how much I loved him in that moment.

We hear the rumble of a pick-up truck coming towards us, I pull Larry up off the ground and we get in the car. Luckily the power door locks still work.

Before sundown we pull into Mike Tholl's rustic cabin, Mike had sold the farm in Tennessee and moved to an abandoned ski lodge in Appalachia. Larry and Mike were reunited one last time.

Mike fed us Beef Bourguignonne and sauteed spinach and we talked about old times. Mike told me where to find the Glory Holes at the college in Boone. I had yet to find true love, but I felt love as Larry and I carved pumpkins with a neighbor's daughter.

Amazingly, these hillbillies did not flinch at Larry's flamboyance, nor at his decaying health. Unlike the supposedly more sophisticated people in Florida, they were not afraid of catching it just by being close to Larry.

Bo Frieden | CHAPTER 31

Mike Tholl's old friend Bo Frieden had an air of intrigue, like a Jewish James Bond. He led us to believe he was Mossad. He would have been in his mid-fifties, when I met him in the late seventies. He was one of the four Old-Timers on the volleyball court at West Street Beach.

He had the presence of a winning football coach. He was deeply tanned and gym toned. His steely brown eyes appraised me when I approached him at age 18 and asked to get in on a game.

"You're asking the right man. I'm the one who sunk these posts, when the city redeveloped Main Beach." The other old timers rolled their eyes.

"Spare me."

"While these Bitches were whimpering in their Tea at Dante's, I singlehandedly moved the gay beach to West Street."

It was shocking to hear Bo call the other middle-aged men "bitches" in his deep, masculine baritone.

Since World War II, Dante's and Barefoot were the two gay bars that sat on the sand in Downtown Laguna. Homosexuals trekked to this artist's colony to soak up the sun and cruise the sailors just returning from overseas. Soon homosexuals from overseas were coming to Laguna. To weed out these undesirables, the city condemned the row of shacks to redevelop the area into the Main Beach boardwalk.

"When the bulldozers came, I took the nets and posts to this deserted cove beyond Camel Point."

This deserted cove, West Street Beach, was now packed with thousands of gay men in popsicle-colored speedos.

"You can thank me for all this!" Bo gestured grandly at the lively beach, sailing yachts bobbing in the blue cove.

"Bitch, Please," Dan Downs took offense at Bo's grandiosity.

Dan was tall and lanky like a high school history teacher. He was freckled and probably had red hair when he still had hair. I sensed calling another man bitch did not come easily to Dan. Which only underscored his weariness at hearing Bo's tall tale. Despite this, Dan was warm and welcoming. Unlike the next man who introduced himself.

"I'm Ron Rudderow," said the most reticent of the four.

He loomed physically large and had a quiet authority. Ron never warmed to me over the years. He was a noted pianist and did not genuflect to youth.

The fourth man certainly appreciated youth, "You can be on my team!" he said, noticing I stood 6'3"."

"I'm Lee." Lee had the pale timidity of an accountant. I played with Lee most every day that first summer and never got his last name.

Most of the men of their generation were fearful of giving last names. Before Stonewall,tThese men had had to live with entrapment. Only 10 years earlier they could have been arrested for being gay. They risked losing their jobs, apartments and could end up in jail, just for dancing with another man.

Bo Frieden and these men taught me how to win at volleyball over that endless summer.

Bo had a bum knee.

"I injured it on the seven mile bridge in Key West racing my Austin-Healey against two flyboys on Kawasakis."

I wondered if this were another of Bo's tall tales.

By 1978 Bo drove a blue Lotus Europa. One night he raced me out Laguna Canyon Road. There was the most beautiful blonde boy riding shotgun naked. Running side by side, Bo glanced at me in triumph. (He was about to overtake my Camaro and he had the son of the Huntington Beach Fire Chief bare-assed naked beside him. He was winning.) While smirking at me, Bo didn't see the orange cones, and his Lotus Europa bounced along the torn-up section of the Canyon Road. Kenny Thornton got a rougher ride than he was hoping for.

Whether Bo's tale was true, he did have a bum knee and was still one hell of a volleyball player.

"Just pass the ball to me. Don't make me move."

Bo wanted the ball passed directly to where he was already heading. Changing directions in mid run would throw out his knee and we would miss the point. If you got the ball to him, exactly where he wanted it, he would always score, Bo had excellent ball placement which made up for his inability to jump and spike the ball. He could dink it short right over the net or shoot it deep to the backline, always catching the other team off guard. Nothing was more satisfying than watching Scott Nelson dive in the sand and miss the ball completely. I credit Bo Frieden for the quality of my ball control that has allowed me to compete up and down the California coast.

Like Eve Harrington, as my skills improved, my ambition forced the old-timers to the sidelines.

I now had my pick of players. More often than not, I'd pick them based on attractiveness. If I couldn't get Kenny Thornton naked in my car, I'd pick Grady Wiley to play ball with me. Grady Wiley was a good looking, well-built Texan new to Laguna, and was considered that summer's hottest number. I had determined that Grady would make a perfect boyfriend for me. Grady had decided I would be the ideal roommate.

After we returned from our Cross-country road trip, I was asked to move out of Donnie's Dana Point condo. I was desperate for a place to live. Grady had rented a modern post and beam apartment behind the Cottage Restaurant in North Laguna. He needed someone to split the rent. Turns out I was ideal as I did not have any furniture of my own. Grady did not want a roommate to bring their tacky sofas into his impeccable modern living room with its two Barcelona chairs.

Grady was about my age, but much more sophisticated. He explained to me that Mies van der Rohe designed the chairs for the 1929 World's Fair in Barcelona. Grady had arranged these two chairs facing each other across a table balancing an orchid. These chairs floated in a large living room that could have held four tacky sofas. There was no TV. Grady insisted that we only have one bed in the bedroom. This sounded logical to my 21-year-old brain, given his monastic design aesthetic. It didn't make sense to my 21-year-old loins.

I lay awake in exquisite agony while Grady slept soundly beside me stark naked. I memorized the curves of his chest and thighs.

Bo and I commiserated over roommates, Bo had to take a roommate named Ralph to share expenses in his home at Top of the World high above Bluebird Canyon, there were so many gay neighbors it was referred to as the "Swish Alps." Although Ralph didn't make Bo sleep in his bed, Ralph curtailed Bo's infamous Everclear parties.

Bo's taste in furniture was even more refined than Grady's. Bo had exquisite white velvet sofas that faced each other across a table with a crystal obelisk. The sofas were designed by his friend, Billy Haines, an exiled Hollywood actor turned decorator. According to Bo, Billy was arrested in a YMCA in 1933 with a sailor he picked up on leave. The studio demanded he enter a lavender marriage, Billy Haines refused and was drummed out of Hollywood and started a decorating business. Joan Crawford championed Billy's designs and launched his successful second act. I'm guessing Bo liked Billy's designs for the same reason as La Crawford. Billy's low-slung furniture made its owner appear larger than life.

Despite being in reduced circumstances, Bo Frieden was larger than life. He only stood 5'10", but he appeared as tall as Paul Bunyan, as did his tales.

He fought in the Israeli war of Independence in 1948, flying B-29 bombers, or so he said.

He told us he'd made and lost fortunes buying and selling Oil Leases in Texas in the 1950's and 1960's.

He took a penthouse in New York City and entertained on a grand scale. Rock Hudson, Christine Jorgensen, Martha Raye all sat on those divine sofas.

Bo pointed out a red wine stain on the white velvet, "Judy Garland spilled her drink."

He took legendary lovers, "Charlie Brown was the first Mrs. Frieden." I was disappointed when I finally met Charlie Brown on West Street Beach. I think I expected to meet the Peanuts character then appearing on Broadway.

"The second Mrs. Frieden, Darko," was a wrestler with an equally unlikely name.

When I met Bo he was on the hunt for the, "Next Mrs. Frieden." Prospects had to be young, hairless and circumcised. I only saw Bo as an old man.

"Beggers can't be choosers," I'm afraid I said out loud. Bo dismissed me with a shake of his head. "And. He can't be tattooed."

Having slept next to a naked Grady Wiley, I knew first hand that he checked each of Bo's boxes, so I introduced them. I overheard their conversation while I played volleyball. As payback for my blue balls, I no longer picked Grady to play volleyball with me.

"I'm from Dallas!" I heard Grady interject.

Bo had spent the years after New York City in San Antonio. I was certain Bo was repeating a story I had heard many times. Bo had claimed to have introduced the H. R. Pufnstuf character to the national stage.

"I met Sid and Marty Krofft when I flew for Braniff," Grady said of the puppeteers who created H.R Pufnstuf.

"My roommate the Trolley Dolly," I sneered from the volleyball court.

This was the first I heard that Grady Wiley was a flight attendant. Knowing this about Grady will help me get a good night's sleep. Although I had yet to work a real job, I somehow felt superior to a flight attendant. At 20 I did not want a flight attendant boyfriend. I still wanted a surfer.

While he was in San Antonio in the mid 1960's, Bo supposedly made his next fortune through HemisFair68. The 1968 World's Fair. Men on the make all know there is money to be made when taxpayer money is being spent. Bo understood the sweet little deals that could be made to set yourself up. He claimed to be the one who brought Sid & Marty Krofft on board to develop the mascot for the fair, a dragon which later was renamed H.R. Pufnstuf and became a Saturday Morning Cartoon.

I was never certain if this was another of Bo's tall tales. I was certain that Grady had no interest in becoming the next Mrs. Frieden. He walked away to seduce a new arrival on the beach.

I had our bed to myself for the next week. With the apartment empty I decided to snoop around to unearth the secrets of my new roommate. I found a picture of Grady in a DC-8 jet wearing his Braniff uniform. He really filled out the tan Halston uniform in all the right places. I changed my mind about a stewardess boyfriend. Stuck to this photo was a picture of a bare-chested Grady Wiley in a leather harness. Now, I will never get another night's sleep.

At 20, I was very intimidated by the leather community of the gay world. I thought they were disgusting, spanking and peeing on each other. Then, I found the book on Grady's bookshelf. Mr. Benson. An erotic novel signed by the author, "To Grady with ties that bind." Gross, my roommate must be into this kinky stuff.

We returned from our road trip to find Bo with the third Mrs. Frieden.

Bobby was a teenage hillbilly from bumfuck nowhere, and was now living with Bo at Lagunita, five houses away from Ozzie and Harriett, and my friend Cori.

Bo could afford to live in this gated enclave because he and Dan Downs had just gone public with an electronic trivia and sports game that could be played in bars. It was called NTN.

Bo had met Bobby the night Bo came with us to the first circuit party called The Mothership Arrives, held at Griffith Observatory. Michael Rotella was one of the promoters.

At almost sixty, Bo had taken the same new hallucinatory drug that we all did, called Ecstacy. He found Bobby sitting alone in a tree and at 60-something Bo had climbed the tree to watch The Ritchie Family perform on the spaceship from *Close Encounters of the Third Kind* that was suspended from a helicopter over the outdoor dancefloor.

This is one Bo story I know to be true, because I was there! Or was I? I came-to the next day at Cedars-Sinai hospital. My friends admitted me because I was spinning around on someone's front lawn unable to stop.

"You told us you were too wound up and had to unwind."

Joseph Genna | CHAPTER 32

Joseph Genna was the personification of the 1980's in Los Angeles. A quiet, weak-chinned farm boy from Madison Wisconsin. He reinvented himself as a celebrity hairdresser in Beverly Hills.

He was a man-about-town in Boystown, which is how West Hollywood was known before it was incorporated as a city in 1984. He lived in an apartment complex on Larrabee.

"It's the first city with a gay mayor!" Joseph would crow

"And, the first city with a Colt Coverman as a City Councilman!" his best friend Juan Cruz would triumphantly one up his pal.

Colt man turned Councilman Steve Schulte was an obsession between these two frenemies.

"She was nicer, before she had that chin implant," Juan would bitchily confide.

"Who, Steve Schulte?," I would naively ask.

"No, child. Miss Thing here," he'd point at Joseph.

"Jo Jo Star," Joseph's handsome face would turn red.

With hard work and determination, Joseph became a hairdresser to the stars in Beverly Hills. To celebrate his new success and new chin, Joseph bought himself a brand-new Triumph TR-8. The wedge -shaped sports car was considered, "The shape of things to come," in Wisconsin. Joseph wanted everyone to know it was Jo Jo's TR. With his newfound confidence, he'd sprung for a vanity license plate "JOJOSTR."

"Miss Thing would be driving home from work on S & M Boulevard, thinking she was hot shit." Juan loved to deflate his friend. "Her layered hair was blowing in the wind, wearing her best Armani she thought she was Richard Gere in *American Gigolo*. Well," Juan continued to his friend's annoyance, "She'd pass the Sports Erection (as Juan referred to the massive WeHo gym named the Sports Connection.) The muscle queens would shout, 'Hey girl, it's Jo Jo Star!'" They would bastardize his personalized plate. Juan concluded his story about how Joseph got his nickname.

I met Joseph in the summer of 1984, by then he was known as Mister Joseph in the Los Angeles Herald-Examiner.

The personalized plate was long gone, as was the TR-8. Joseph was now driving a brand-new C-4 Corvette. He didn't make the mistake of getting a vanity plate for this car.

I met Joseph Genna and Juan Cruz in Laguna Beach when I was standing in the street outside The Coast Inn after last call at the Boom Boom Room. The street was as crowded as Times Square on New Year's Eve.

Just like New York City when the ball drops, In Laguna Beach these boys were looking for someone to kiss. Before, I would not be caught dead standing alone in this street, but all my friends had been lost to AIDS. I was alone and lonely, so I joined the hoi polloi cruising for a man.

"*A real man, a good man, a true man. A man to love me for sure.*" I could hear the voice of my lost friend Stevie B reciting Bette Midler's monologue from *The Rose*.

My reverie was interrupted by two sexy dark-haired men at my elbows. "Want a bump?" One of them asked.

"Want a blow job?" asked the other.

I wanted both, but I said, "No, thank you." In 1984, I still imagined I had a spotless reputation to protect.

"Are you with friends?" Joseph asked, possessively clutching my elbow. "We've got a room upstairs." He said, trying to propel me to the stairs that led to the motel rooms above the bar at the Coast Inn.

I was seriously considering accepting this invitation to a menage a trois.

"I've never seen the rooms here." I heard myself saying.

Juan broke away from us in a huff My tequila-infused brain suspected I was causing a lover's quarrel.

"Neat!" Joseph pleaded as Juan pushed through the crowd.

"I'm going to the beach." Juan replied taking off his shirt. This got everyone's attention. Soon there was a parade heading down the steps to the beach. Now, Joseph and I were the one of the few left standing in the street.

"Neat is short for Juanita." Joseph explained as he settled me onto a chaise on the oceanfront terrace to their suite.

It was getting cold on the terrace of the Coast Inn in the wee small hours of the morning. Demonstrating his thoughtfulness as a host, Joseph Genna brought out an extra blanket and arranged it around both of us. The only sound to be heard was the gentle lapping of the surf on the beach below us, mingling with the occasional sniff of cocaine. A waxing moon cast shadows of the men cruising the beach below. I tried to pick out Joseph's friend Juan among the shadows. I still didn't know the status of Joseph's relationship with Juan. I spotted what looked to be a short man of about Juan's stature, on his knees next to a taller man.

"Is that Neat?" trying out Juan's nickname I pointed to the shadows of the men on the beach. No sooner, had I pointed them out to Joseph, than the shorter man popped up from his knees like a jack in the box, as the tide engulfed them. Obviously neither was Juan. Joseph seemed unconcerned.

"Let's make a fort!" Joseph said pulling the covers over our head in delight. The Beverly Hills hairdresser reverted to the Madison dairy farmer, as he tried to cop a feel and steal a kiss. Joseph had an instinct for timing as the sensual ballet we'd been watching on the beach below had aroused me.

"Girl!" Juan exclaimed as he pulled the covers off us, effectively destroying our fort. "Are you playing dairy farmer again?" He teased Joseph. "I need a bump!" he demanded.

Juan had a tall blonde man in tow, a nemesis of mine from the volleyball court on West Street beach. As they passed Joseph's vial between each other, Juan made the introductions.

"Nevermind!" the tall blonde said. "I know that trash," he said pointing to me. And this must be "Jo Jo Star," he mocked, extending a big hairy paw to Joseph.

I protectively pulled Joseph away from the proffered hand, angry that the big blonde had cruelly reminded Joseph of his hated nickname.

"Don't touch it! You don't know where that hand has been." I said.

"Oh My!" Joseph vamped, rolling his shoulders like Mae West, "playing hand ball?"

This was my cue to gather myself and leave. Whatever was about to go down with these LA Boys was too sophisticated for me. As I used the bathroom, I could hear Joseph telling Juan, "Nothing happened. He's a good boy. Doesn't put out on the first date, which means he is holding out for a serious relationship.'

"Girl, you are nuttier than a fruitcake." I heard Juan say as I left the suite.

Joseph Genna saw the world through rose-tinted glasses. Instead of accepting things as they are, he saw them as he wanted them to be.

He saw my refusal to stay and party differently than I saw it. I saw cocaine and casual sex in a seedy room above a gay bar as a sure way to contract GRID (before AIDS it was called Gay Related Immuno-Deficiency).

Joseph saw it differently, he saw my reticence as that of "a good boy, holding out for true love." (If any of my friends were still alive, they would tell you I was anything but a good boy. Duff Paddock would tell you, that I had my own vial stashed in the coin pocket of my 501s, so I wasn't beholden to anyone by taking their bump. Donnie McPhedran would be too happy to tell you about my own nights, lurking in the shadows on the beach).

Just as Joseph could see a dairy farmer becoming a highly paid Beverly Hills hairdresser, he saw me and him as boyfriends.

I had promised myself I would never date a hairdresser. I swore I would never set foot in WeHo.

But, soon I was driving my VW Thing to Beverly Hills.

We made an incongruous couple, a 6'3" blonde beach boy with a 5'8" Italian hairdresser. But odd couples were all the rage in the early 1980's. Rocky, Sly Stallone, had left his wife for Golden Girl Susan Anton, who towered over him.

Joseph was always on-trend. He knew all the best restaurants and the hottest clubs. He was where you should be all the time.

Our second date was the penultimate 80's Los Angeles experience. Joseph took me to an aerobics class.

"This is not your typical Valley Girl's aerobics class." Joseph told me condescendingly. "This Isn't even the tourist trap that Jane

Fonda's Workout on Robertson has become." What this was, or was supposed to be, was, "Ground Zero for the Beautiful People." Joseph took me to Karen Voight's studio when it was between Alfred and La Cienega in West Hollywood.

"Matt Collins and all the playmates work out here," Joseph boasted. "Karen always saves a spot for me! It's packed with famous faces. You'll be the only unknown." Joseph breathlessly continued. "I'm taking you to All American Boy for new work out gear!" Like a Ken Doll, Joseph outfitted me in the newest Reeboks with slouchy socks, ridiculous neon shorts and a skimpy tank. The only famous face I recognized at the Voight studio was the woman who played the receptionist on the first *Bob Newhart Show*. The lanky, flame-haired second banana was doing the pelvic thrust right next to me.

I was sweating buckets. All the other guys in class had ripped their shirts off by now.

We were doing drop kicks and forward lunges to a high energy song I had never heard before.

"This is the new Bonnie Tyler song," Joseph shouted to me while we were doing sidekicks. "It was written by the guy in the first row in the blue-striped Dolphin Shorts." Joseph wheezed. " It's going to be on the soundtrack to the new Kevin Bacon movie." Joseph finished out of breath. The guy's name was Dean Pitchford, the movie would be *Footloose*. The song was *Holding Out for a Hero*.

I considered this Our Song.

Joseph was not the only one of us wearing rose-colored glasses.

I thought of this affair as a summer fling.

Even though it began with an Easter Egg hunt at the Playboy Mansion, and ended after a New Years Eve party where I sulked in a rented tux, between two of Joseph's celebrity clients, Season Hubley (who stole my heart in 6th grade when she played a runaway princess on the Partridge Family) and Dallas' villainess Cassie Yates.

In my defense, California is an Endless Summer.

Like Truman Capote, Joseph surrounded himself with his swans. Joseph's swans were his celebrity clients like Vanna White, Deidre Hall, Season Hubley and so on down through random guest stars on *The Love Boat*. My favorite was Sheila Caan (James Caan's ex-wife and the mother of Scott Caan.) Sheila was an It Girl who once dated Elvis.

Eventually, as if looking through corrective lenses, Joseph and I saw this thing clearly and we transitioned. Like thousands of homosexuals before us, we went from tricks to friends.

Joseph Genna was a very good friend to me when I had to leave Laguna. I took my first job at an advertising agency in Los Angeles. He got me a gig housesitting for a girlfriend of his, Michelle, while she was in Australia. They both lived at the Mid-Century Sweetzer Lanai just off Fountain. He welcomed me into his circle of friends. Gay friendship circles in the 80's were as incestuous as Fleetwood Mac. Not only was I included, but Juan often brought his ex, the talent agent Billy Miller.

Joseph would frequently chastise Juan, "You're not bringing that Nasty Old Billy, are you?"

On nights when Joseph wasn't swanning around with his swans, he had his assistant call each of us, "Church, Joseph would like you to join him and some friends at Marix, Tex-Mex at 5:00 PM sharp."

His assistant addressed me by my nickname, "Church." I often wondered if she addressed Billy Miller as "That Nasty Old Billy."

Joseph curated his dinner guests like a Brat Pack movie. Although many tables at the rowdy Marix were filled with the stars du jour. Joseph's table often sparkled the brightest. If not the brightest we were the loudest.

Joseph may have been a snob, but he was a loyal friend to his first friends in town. Daylee Henderson and Bruce Johnson went to Beauty School with Joseph. They were often included in our nights out at Marix. They were flamboyant black queens who always made an evening that much wilder. Daylee claimed to do a woman from Chicago's hair. He said her name was Oprah Winfrey. At the time, none of us had heard of her. She was on a tiny little station in Chicago called WGN.

Bruce had no such claim to fame. he didn't need one. He stood an imposing 6'4" of solid muscle.

"But! make no mistake, I am a lady!" he would protest.

Bruce could tell one helluva story, "You should have seen this bitch," Bruce began, pointing at Joseph, "upon our graduation, we were required to put in thirty hours behind the chair to get our license."

Securing a cosmetology license in California is not an easy undertaking. It is even more difficult to get your first job, you must start out as an assistant to a stylist, which is akin to being an apprentice to Satan.

"The only place that would hire us, was that mortuary on La Brea." Bruce took a gulp of his kick-ass margarita. Joseph glared daggers at him. "This bitch was doing a blow out on a late sister's textured hair."

"That bitch's hair," Joseph interjected, "was kinkier and nappier than either of these two bitches!" Joseph said indicating Daylee and Bruce.

Juan and I both did a Charlies Angels' hair flip with our luxurious tresses. This brought the entire table to tears of laughter. Except for That Nasty Old Billy who was not amused.

"I said, Girl, pull the brush harder! Just yank it!" Joseph blushed with embarrassment. To straighten curly hair you have to maintain tension by stretching the hair with a round brush. "Yank it! It's not like the bitch can feel it. She's dead!" Bruce Johnson finished his roast of Joseph.

Joseph worked his way up the ladder to be the top Colorist at Allen Edwards Salon on Rodeo Drive. He famously did Vanna White's hair when she was the most famous woman in America. He also did Patti D'Arbanville's hair when she appeared at the Oscars with her then-boyfriend Don Johnson, at the height of the *Miami Vice* hysteria.

Bruce Johnson was the first person I knew to get sick with AIDS. I accompanied Joseph to Midway Hospital to visit. This was the scariest thing I ever did, we all assumed that we were carrying the virus ourselves. At this point in the mid 1980's nobody was certain how the virus was transmitted. The head nurse refused to allow us admittance to Bruce's room. She was physically escorting us off the floor. I could see Bruce in his hospital bed. He was as emaciated as the cadavers at Auschwitz.

"The only visitors we allow are next of kin," the nurse firmly informed us. I could hear Bruce croak, "These bitches are my sisters, that makes them next of kin." I noticed a flicker of a smile on nurse Ratched. Joseph was always aware of a window of opportunity.

"I'll do your hair on Rodeo Drive, if you please let us visit our sister."

Soon we were in hazmat suits sitting at Bruce's bedside. His face looked like a skull, his body was skin and bones. I found it impossible to look at him. His face and arms were covered with the tell-tale purple blotches of Kaposi's Sarcoma cancer, they were covered in some kind of makeup.

Bruce noticed me staring. "Girl," he addressed Joseph, "it's impossible to find a concealer to match a Black Girls' skin!" He took a rattled breath. "When I get out of here, I'm going to start a cosmetic line just for us black girls. I'll be richer than that Tova Borgnine."

This broke my heart. I recognized that Bruce was never going to get out of that hospital. A muscular orderly entered the room, carrying a circular plastic bag filled with blood.

"Who wants pizza?" Bruce asked. The blood bag did resemble a large cheeseless pizza. "This is my favorite time of day," Bruce said batting his eyelids at the orderly as he hooked up the bag to the drip. "The Pizza Man, He Delivers!" Bruce campily enunciated the title of a hit gay porn movie. I'd forgotten the sound of laughter.

Joseph Genna's and my friendship began to disintegrate after Joseph berated me for not attending Bruce Johnson's funeral. Instead, I went to the beach on a sunny Santa Ana day. Joseph didn't allow for my reasoning, Bruce Johnson was his friend, not mine. At only 26 I understood that I would soon be attending the funerals of my own friends. I wasn't sure that I would not be next.

Joseph didn't speak to me for months, until Juan got sick.

Joseph continued to treat me coolly throughout Juan's illness. He never forgave me for not attending Bruce Johnson's funeral. Joseph was frosty to me whenever our paths crossed, whether it was in a hospital or a hospice.

Juan's friend Billy Miller was a devoted caregiver, "That Nasty Old Billy," was by Juan's side constantly.

Since I lived next door to Juan, in his old studio apartment, I kept him company regularly. "I haven't seen that old bitch, Joseph." Juan would commiserate. "She's got that 'Benson Bug'."

Through it all we made light of the business of dying. Joseph had been diagnosed with Guillain-Barre syndrome. Typically, the two of them, made up a joke about it. They mistakenly thought it was Guillaume, like the actor on the sitcom Benson.

Looking back, I can see we didn't dive deep into our health journey. Around the time Juan was battling AIDS, the drug AZT became available. I am not sure if he was taking it. Juan never admitted his condition with me. By this time the Elisa test for HIV became available. Like many of us who came of age in the hedonism of the late 1970's, I just assumed I had it. I was hesitant to get the test. Watching the disease ravage Juan and witnessing the decline in Joseph. Because there was no treatment, I didn't see the upside in knowing that I will get sick and die.

By now, Juan was suffering night sweats. One morning I went over and stripped his bed to wash his sheets. I was very conscious of the affront to Juan of my slipping my hands into latex gloves (we still weren't certain how it was transmitted). The simple act of putting on gloves acknowledged the unspoken.

I decided to confront the truth head on.

I made an appointment at The Center in Long Beach to have my blood drawn anonymously. At this time in the mid-1980's anonymity was key. We weren't sure if our insurance carriers would cancel us. People were losing their jobs and health coverage. The government was considering quarantining us (remember, it was only a mere thirty years earlier our government shipped American citizens to internment camps during WWII, just because they were Japanese).

After many sleepless nights, my HIV test came back negative. I had no one to share my good news with. I couldn't flaunt my good luck to my dying friends. This secret drove a further wedge into our friendship.

My friendship with Joseph was already complicated. Beyond the fact that we once dated, I was still a provincial small-town boy clinging to antiquated values. I tried to anchor Joseph to the midwestern values he fled from long ago. I much preferred the farm boy under a fort of blankets to the celebrity hairdresser under an armor of Armani. Now, I can see how Joseph found me tiresome, I do too.

Like the Wisconsin winters he abhorred, Joseph froze me out in favor of two new A-List Gays. Despite Juan's increasingly fragile condition, Joseph insisted on hosting a birthday party for him at the trendiest restaurant at that moment in time. We all put on coats and ties to gather at Le Restaurant on Melrose Place to celebrate what I suspected would be Juan's last birthday.

I find it hard to look at this picture of us. Juan had just recovered from a bout with Bell's Palsy that left him with a facial droop. That "Nasty Old Billy," stands in the back. Joseph's new best friends Marc and Thom are circling like vultures, ready to help ease the burden of furniture and artwork. An International Male underwear model adds a touch of class to this tableau.

Joseph's gift to his best friend Juan was an all-expense paid trip to Hawaii.

I could see Billy marshalling his protest that, "Juan is too sick to make the trip." But we both noticed the childlike delight on Juan's face and nothing was said.

Except Marc & Thom spoke up, "We'd be happy to housesit while you're in paradise."

I had no gift to give Juan. I was incapable of shopping for the appropriate gift for a dying friend. I had wandered through the Beverly Center like Maureen Stapleton in the movie *Airport*, walking blindly through tears and leaning against walls for support.

This absence of a gift did not go unnoticed by Joseph, who oohed and aahed over the Vuitton checkbook cover gifted by Marc

& Thom. ("The perfect gift for someone about to buy the farm," I wanted to say.)

Juan and Joseph had a fabulous time in Waikiki. I hooked them up with my friend Peter Lyle who put their name on the list at Wave Waikiki. This trip invigorated them both. They came back with hysterical stories and videos. That Nasty Old Billy had given Juan a video camera for his birthday. It was as big as a bazooka.

There was a video of the aftermath of a night out at the Wave Waikiki. Juan dressed head to toe in White Linen. His beautiful clothes were in tatters, sleeves were ripped off, bright red splotches of blood dotted the fabric.

"This big Samoan bouncer picked me up in the air and threw me out the door," Juan said with glee.

"Neat was hitting on him." Joseph interjected.

"Now watch this!" Juan demanded, excitedly.

The video showed a sandy foot, bleeding from a deep gash, in a bathtub at the Royal Hawaiian hotel.

"I had to pee on Miss Thing," Juan giddily went on. "I cut my foot on some coral," Joseph soberly explained. The two friends dissolved into tears of laughter. Billy and I just dissolved into tears.

Juan was dead before the year ended.

There was a memorial service and interment at Forest Lawn in Glendale.

Joseph did not attend. He chose to vacation on Fire Island.

Just as Joseph had frozen me out for skipping Bruce Johnson's funeral, I ended my friendship with him for missing Juan's. Forty years later, I see now, I took the easy way out from watching another friend die.

Since Joseph valued his A-List Gays more than me, I thought, *they can take care of him.* Childish, I know. But I was little more than a child when everyone was dying.

That Nasty Old Billy stuck around and took care of Joseph until the very end.

Billy Miller and I were the only mourners I recognized from Joseph's glamorous life. A funeral mass was held at St. Victors in West Hollywood.

Joseph used to call it St. Victor/Victoria's after the Julie Andrews cross-dressing film. Because there were so many homosexuals in the congregation of this Boy's Town church. Praying for their lives.

Juan Cruz | CHAPTER 33

Juan Cruz was an easy guy to be friends with. He was handsome, funny and was always up for doing things. For 8 years he was my neighbor on West Knoll Drive in West Hollywood. In fact, I inherited his old studio apartment when he moved up in the world to a one-bedroom. I also inherited his old tricks who would come knocking on the door after the bars had closed. Juan was unabashedly sexual.

"You're still closeted," he'd chastise me. I thought I was out and proud.

"You're a closet slut." He saw my shameful secret.

Rumors swirled that he had done a porn loop back in the days before VHS under the name Mike Cole. He proudly went to the 8709 and Basic Plumbing.

Juan Cruz fit in anywhere. He was equally at home in black tie for HRC fundraisers at Duke Comegys as he was at a backyard barbecue at Allee Willis's. "The Del Rubio triplets were there!" "Kitten Natividad jumped on a trampoline!" Juan would gush to Joseph. "Can you I. Magnin?"

Juan made custom furniture to the trade. His new apartment was a showplace. His coffee table was a slab of pink marble repurposed from the new Palm Spring's hotel Maxim's.

"Ron Wilson, Cher's designer got it for me."

Along with the hairy men coming to my door, Juan left behind a linen covered parson's table. A prized possession I kept for 30 years.

Juan knew everybody. He was a magnetic personality in the early 1980's. Juan and Joseph helped make Marix Tex-Mex on Flores the most popular gay restaurant in town.

Marix was an old Spanish bungalow packed to the rafters with models and aerobics instructors. To tell the truth, it did not have rafters as the roof was removed from the place, creating LA's first indoor-outdoor dining. If it had had a roof, the rowdy crowd would have raised the roof with their antics. Fueled by $11.00 pitchers of "Kick-Ass Margaritas," the place was teetering on the forbidden like a drag queen in high heels. Marix was packed so tight that waiting patrons would be standing right next to your table.

You'd be eating sizzling fajitas rolled into a flour tortilla with the most magnificent buns in your face. At a certain point in the evening flour tortillas would be tossed through the room like Frisbees with phone numbers scrawled on them.

"Church, give me that one. You've already caught six tonight." The advantage of standing over six feet.

"C'mon," Joseph pleaded, "I'll buy a pack of matches tonight."

In the wild west of Tex Mex, a waiter would ask if you wanted desert, if you said "the usual, please" a paper Marix matchbook would arrive stuffed with a bindle, the cost for the blow would appear on your check as a Service Fee

Once the plates were cleared, "five and under" actors would begin dancing on tables. You'd notice "above the title" actors slip out once things got out of control. I'd seen Madonna, Courtney Cox and Vanna White all enjoying Marix margaritas.

Juan's wit was deliciously deadly. He had hilarious nicknames for every denizen of the nascent city of West Hollywood. "Isn't that your boyfriend Amanda Bellows?" Juan would needle me.

I was besotted with a boy who was kept by Hayden Rorke, the actor who played Doctor Bellows on *I Dream of Jeannie*.

Whenever one of the city's most notorious hustlers arrived at Marix, Juan would hum Lohengrin's *Bridal March*. The procession of this rent boy would drive Joseph to hysterics.

"Here cums the Bride," Joseph would explain to anyone within earshot, "she's got more stitches than the bride of Frankenstein. That's how much work she's had done."

"Well, somebody sewed a dick of death on her," Juan added.

These Dicks of Death were just that.

AIDS was killing so many. Unlike cancer which hides in the cells, AIDS symptoms were painfully visible. Kaposi's Sarcoma dotted the flesh with purple spots, like port wine stains. Facial wasting made the scull look like a cadaver. Crix Belly and Buffalo hump deformed the body with fat deposits like the Elephant Man. Yet these brave men went about their daily lives defiantly while so many turned away in fear.

I was ever alert to these symptoms in my friends. In those early days when a diagnosis was a death sentence, we didn't share our diagnosis.

Fatigue and a dry cough were the first warning signs. One never canceled plans claiming they were too tired. They did a bump of coke and went to Probe to keep up appearances.

When I first met Juan he had a Studebaker Lark. He and his ex-boyfriend Billy Miller loved the cars from South Bend—Billy had a 1950 Champion. Juan and I bonded over cars, we were always working on cars together. We customized them per our personal tastes. When Juan ordered his red Jeep CJ-7, he specced the hard doors and the bikini top.

Before he showed it to his ex-boyfriend Billy, he wanted to remove the tape stripes that came with it. We borrowed a professional strength blow-drier from Joseph. One heated the stripe until the adhesive was loose, and then you pulled the stripe off. It was a two-man job, I ran the blow dryer while Juan peeled the stripe. Feeling unwell on this hot summer day Juan went inside to cool off. He never came back out. I knew in my gut that Juan was sick. Through tears and fears I continued to remove the stripes.

To this day a Jeep with stripes sends a chill up my spine.

Juan was the only friend that I saw get sick and die. One day Bell's Palsy paralyzed the left side of his face. His ex-lover Billy took over as caregiver. I did whatever I was asked. Since I lived just across the street, I was available for emergencies. I appointed myself as the Normalizer. I'd try to do things with Juan that he usually liked to do. One day we went to the beach. I braced myself for when he took his shirt off, afraid of what I might see. There were no tell-tale purple splotches. His dark Cuban skin was sallow and gray. His perfect bubble butt was as deflated as my pancake ass. Yet his spirits were high and he was happy to be outside.

Friends hopped from towel to towel across the hot sand of Venice Beach to say hello. Invitations to parties and dinners were extended and accepted.

"Girl, look over there! Is that that hot new Aussie actor who replaced the love of my life Jon-Erik Hexum?"

What is said about rattlesnakes was true about my friend Juan Cruz, "The last thing to die is the tail."

In his waning days he took a new boyfriend. I don't remember his name. This made it awkward when I came over in the morning to launder the sheets. Juan soaked them with night sweats. I thought it was brave of this boyfriend to sleep with Juan when it was painfully obvious that he was so ill. Courage that I didn't have. I had ceased looking for a boyfriend when every other gay man was dying of AIDS.

Somehow Juan continued to work. His mother came to stay with him. We were encouraged to stay away. Her Toyota Celica took the parking spot where his Jeep used to be. Juan had sold it. A stinging admission that things had changed. Still Juan never discussed his illness with me. Turns out we gays pioneered, *"Don't Ask, Don't Tell"* long before it was usurped by the military.

Things changed quickly. One morning Juan got out of bed and fell headfirst through his new standing floor length mirror. Billy took him to the hospital. Waiting for news, I busied myself to keep from screaming. I picked up the glass shards and scrubbed the blood out of the new Berber carpeting. Juan had redecorated his apartment with the proceeds from the Jeep sale. He had commissioned Allee Willis an 80's creative force in LA to do a piece of artwork titled Vintage Habana.

"It was the neuropathy," Billy explained. Billy also explained they would be moving Juan to the Chris Brownlie Hospice in Echo Park.

To combat my despair, I set about making a list of things to do. The first thing to do was to buy a car so I could make the commute to Echo Park. In a fog I had sold my Barracuda Convertible and begun taking public buses. I had missed the lesson in Missing Person's *Walking in LA*.

I think I believed I wouldn't be able to run away without a car.

The Santa Ana winds blew early that fall. My new car, a 17-year-old AMC Hornet, didn't have air conditioning. I'd arrive at the hospice looking as sweaty and sickly as the patients after the long drive out the Glendale Freeway.

"Church, you're a mess, fix yourself up!" Juan would say in lieu of hello.

I made the trip for two weeks just to sit by his bed. I recognized many faces from Marix walking the corridors. I'd leave when Billy Miller arrived.

Billy made the arrangements at Forest Lawn in Glendale. I stood outside sweating in my blue blazer, distressed over what Juan would have thought. The other mourners were perspiring as well. The day was hotter than the hinges of hell. We could see the men cruising the bushes at nearby Griffith Park. The memorial was moved inside into the air conditioned chapel. TV starlets skipped barefoot to the podium to remember Juan. Juan Cruz would have loved it. Juan's best friend, Joseph was a no-show. He had chosen to keep his plans to vacation on Fire Island. I noticed other mourners in their shiny Mercedes head over to cruise Griffith Park after the service.

"The last thing to die is the tail"

New Kid In Town | CHAPTER 34

It was the early 1980's and I was the new kid in town. I had just moved from Laguna Beach to West Hollywood, which at the time was still a town, not yet a city. At that time, it was referred to as, "Boystown."

I was literally a fish out of water. For the past eight years I had been steeped in the sensuality of saltwater. Now I had to wear clothes. I was embarking on my first job in Advertising. For $325 a month I had rented a studio apartment just below the Sunset Strip. I was alone in the big city. I was taken up by two young gay men about town, Juan Cruz and Joseph Genna, dark-haired lads about half my height. With little else in common we loved cars and carousing. Juan was a smoldering Cuban who drove a Studebaker and made custom furnishings for "the trade."

Joseph was an Italian from Wisconsin who was a Beverly Hills Hairdresser, he had just bought himself a brand new C4 Corvette, he had the first one in town. Since they were already on their way and I was just starting out, I could not afford to keep up with their social schedule.

Weekend nights saw me at home microwaving a Stauffer's frozen dinner. Besides being poor, I was also saving myself for true love.

As Joseph would say, "He may look like sex-on-a-stick, but he is more like a popsicle. Frigid."

When the telephone rang that Saturday evening, I let my answering machine pick up, so people would think I was out enjoying the big city, "Girrrl, I know you're home. Pick up!, It's your fairy godmother."

"Hello Joseph." I said when I picked up the receiver. I hated the gay way of calling each other girl, I was going to assert my masculinity, "You might be a fairy," I said, "but just because you're Italian you are not my godmother."

Joseph took a long, dramatic inhale, "Church-erella," he said bastardizing my nickname "Church."

"Get up off your knees."

"I beg your pardon," I said all righteous indignation.

"OK, you probably aren't sucking cock. But I know you are scrubbing the kitchen floor." It's true, I was.

"I've got a table for four at Mark's." Joseph continues on his one breath. "I'm hosting a little dinner, hosting means that you don't have to pay! But, I need you to pick up your evil stepsister, Miss Juanita. My Corvette is full already. And I don't want Miss Thing pulling up in her nasty old Studebaker. I can forgive you your Barracuda because it is so butch. And Church, wear shoes. Put yourself together, look sharp, Mark's is the tits. Be there at 8:00."

Luckily, I have a new pair of shoes, K-Swiss is one of the accounts at my job, so I have a new pair of size 12 white leather tennis shoes. I look through the slim pickings in my closet, I spent what little money I had on suits to wear to work, so I don't have much in the way of going out clothes. I have a few Stussy collared shirts which were very stylish for going out to dinner at the beach. I chose the one in psychedelic paisley. I know that Juan and Joseph will just be in jeans, so I look for my 501's. Of course, they are dirty, in the hamper. I put on my gray corduroy Quiks, I know Joseph will shit a brick because they are shorts, but who cares, all the muscle boys in West Hollywood will be wearing tank tops to a fancy dinner to show off their biceps. I can wear short shorts to show off my legs. I run my fingers through my wet hair and jump in my convertible 69 Barracuda Formula S. The 340 V-8 rumbles arousingly as I head to pick up Juan Cruz. Juan just lives across the street on West Knoll Drive. All I need to do to pick him up is drive up my driveway.

  In contrast to Joseph, Juan is earthy and unaffected. He always seems to vibrate with excitement, Joseph affects a "been there, done that" attitude. Juan has dressed for our initial foray to Mark's, he's got on skin-tight shrink-to-fit 501s hugging his little Cuban booty and new boots from Bobby To, and a tight white t-shirt, but what breaks the clone look is a fantastic, fringed leather jacket from Theodore. Like all Latins, Juan's body is constantly undulating but the fringe flapping from his outstretched arms makes him appear a bird in flight.

"Neat," my masculine nickname for Juan, shortened from Joseph's "Juanita" and his later "Nita."

"You look fabulous!" I say.

Juan replies, "Girrrl, you are so gay, I've only been in your car for one minute and you're already dropping the F-word. You don't fool me with your beach drag. Play some Madonna, bitch,"

Juan takes me down a notch. I put on the new True Blue cassette.

"I don't know what Jo Jo Star is up to tonight," Juan wonders aloud what Joseph has planned for tonight's surprise, "I can't I Magnin (Joseph's affected way of saying 'imagine' referencing a chic department store in Beverly Hills) what she is up to tonight… maybe she's gone and bought herself a husband, you only go to Mark's if you want to show off."

I laugh heartily, Joseph is the penultimate consumer.

"Can you I Magnin," he pauses for effect . "Or Jerry or Joseph?" (Jerry Magnin is another boutique as is Joseph Magnin.)

Juan's shtick never fails to amuse me.

We pull up in my Barracuda to the valet stand at a chic white building with low walls topped with Horsetail Grass.

My 15-year old Plymouth is in line behind a couple of new Ferraris, an Aston Martin Volante and a Rolls-Royce Corniche.

"Waldo must be here," Juan says indicating the Rolls. (Waldo Fernandez is the decorator du jour, I'm sorry, "designer," he has just been retained by Merv Griffin to remodel the Beverly

Hilton Hotel. Juan is building a dozen custom credenzas for Waldo for the Cocoanut Grove in the hotel.)

"Yes, Dear, I'm here!" says the handsome head peering through the horsetail grass, separating it like Gladys Kravitz peeping through vertical blinds.

Like a Vegas showgirl I hoist my leg high onto my Barracuda's fender and tie the lace of my new white K-Swiss shoes, pleased to see how tan they make my legs look.

"C'mon, you cheap hooker." Juan says grabbing me by the arm. We walk into the restaurant, which in my memory is all white stucco and cushions, the green Horsetail Grass being the only accent of color.

Against this minimalist design the patrons stand out like Peacocks in their finery. Expensive ensembles undoubtedly purchased from either I, Jerry, or Joseph Magnin.

In most likelihood, they were bought at Maxfield Bleu, the up and comer that will make Juan's old joke passe. We scan the room for Joseph, instead of a hostess we are greeted by Mark himself. Mark made his name as a Maitre d' at Le Restaurant on Melrose Place, which at the time was decorator alley, before the Blue Whale of the Pacific Design Center was built-which explains why the restaurant is crawling with decorators.

"Good Evening, Mr. Cruz," Mark says obsequiously, "you are joining Mr. Genna's table, I presume."

It is refreshing to finally hear a masculine pronoun attached to my friend's names. According to a girlfriend of mine, Brandt, Mark is straight, she should know because they "date" on occasion.

This information never fails to disturb Juan who insists he has heard from '"someone who would know" that Mark is hung like a horse and is not opposed to a blow job from a talented man.

According to my friend Brandt, one of those assertions is not true. Juan and I are escorted to one of the best tables in the house, a banquette on the upper level of the terrace where we have a view of the entire restaurant. More importantly, they have a view of us. I am trailing Juan whose fringed jacket makes him appear a bat in flight, or a fruit fly. Joseph stands up very grandly, he is dressed to kill in an over-the-top Cosby sweater that must be a thousand-dollar Thierry Mugler.

"Vanna, I want you to meet two of my best friends, Juan Cruz and Church."

"I'm David Churchill," I say as I take Vanna White's extended hand.

The game show hostess's smile seems warm and authentic.

"Church, Let go of Vanna's hand," Joseph says. condescendingly. I am so tanned that my blushing doesn't show.

"Can I introduce Mark?" Juan asks Joseph.

"No, Nita," he says while lewdly fondling the peppermill, "Vanna already has her own well-hung restauranteur."

He stands up laughing and high marches in a circle, slapping his legs with mirth, like a wind-up Nutcracker stuck in a corner.

Since Vanna's not tan, I can see her blush bright red. I recall reading that Vanna took up with Linda Evan's ex-beau George Santo-Pietro, who owns a pizza parlor in Westwood by UCLA.

"I envy your tan," Vanna says to me to change the subject. "I grew up in Myrtle Beach and I was always tan like you, but I can't be tan on TV."

Joseph does Vanna's hair.

Like pilgrims seeking a papal audience, Decorators and hairdressers make their way to our table to get a good look at Vanna. She takes my hand to avoid the crush of onlookers.

I take my cue and engage her in conversation, "You should come to Manhattan Beach and hang out with us, under an umbrella of course,"

"My brother, Chip, lives in Playa del Rey," She says.

Joseph will not be deterred from showing off his prized client, "And this is Vanna, and my ex-friend Church." He says pointedly.

I shake hands with the sallow, bitter old decorator shielding Vanna with my back. "I think we've met,' he says to me, accusingly.

I brace myself for the belittling comment I am expecting. I am a young man, but I am not on the make, which confuses these older men who treat young men as commodities, they even call us Twinkies. Since I don't want to be in pictures, or to be kept, these supposedly sophisticated men don't know how to approach me.

"Yes, I remember," he says through parched blue lips, "you were playing that 'lonely new kid in town' act by trolling the aisles of the Vons, with a single, sad frozen dinner in your basket, searching for someone to buy you dinner at a restaurant."

I was taken aback and didn't know how to respond. I thought of mocking him for the way he carried his handbasket, like a handbag slung over his arm. Joseph shoots me a "'be still' look," which just enrages me.

"What did you say your name was?" I ask, Then channeling my friend Duff Paddock. "Obviously, my Hungry Man frozen dinner intimidated you, I need more than a mouthful."

I can feel Vanna pat me on the back.

"I'm Frank Austin," his friend interrupts and everyone re-introduces themselves. "Speaking of the Von's I was just there, Marlee Matlin was in the store and everyone was just whispering to each other and pointing her out."

"And then", a big dramatic breath, "that muscular checker on Aisle 1 gets on the intercom, 'Good evening, Vons shoppers, Your attention please, Oscar Winner Marlee Matlin is in the store,' echoes through the supermarket."

"Oh My God," Juan says, "that bitch is deaf."

"Which bitch?" Joseph asks, "Marlee or the checker, body of Mr. Universe with Eve Arden's face."

He continues, "Church wasn't she one of your tricks?"

Marlee Matlin was the first deaf actress to win the academy award.

The other decorator who belittled me pipes up, disgruntled at being sidelined, "Well," dramatic pause, "I was at that same Von's, near Wes Wheadon's office, and I saw Princess Stephanie pushing a shopping cart. What's the point of being a princess and having to shop at Vons?"

While everyone is gasping, I seek my revenge, "Well, you're a queen shopping at Vons." The waiter brings our meals so the decorators scurry back to their tables.

Joseph is basking in all eyes being on him, "Church you were rude to our friends."

"Let your mother help you with the silverware."

"That fork is for the fish, it is not the salad fork."

"I am using my salad fork." I defend myself. Eyeing the fish fork which is just sitting there. "That fish fork shouldn't even be here as I ordered the Filet Mignon." My friend Mike Tholl taught me silverware etiquette.

Juan pipes up to keep the peace, "Oh, That Frank Austin," Juan starts, "he gave a dinner party in that dreadful condo of his with that mirrored staircase like the one he did for Numbers, and he got Polly Bergen and Babara Walters stoned on Angel Dust."

Uncomfortable with the gossip, Vanna turns to me, "Have you ever been to the Playboy Mansion?"

I shake my head no and smile.

"Well, my boyfriend and I are having a barbecue on Easter Sunday and then we are all going to the mansion for the egg hunt. I hope you can come."

She glances at Joseph. "You can bring Joseph if you want." Graciously, Joseph picks up the check as he promised. We all file out of the restaurant basking in the reflected limelight of the most famous woman in America at that moment in time.

Vanna White just renewed her contract on *Wheel of Fortune* for two more years.

Juan Cruz died of AIDS in 1989 and Joseph Genna the next year.

Fade Away And Radiate | CHAPTER 35

I never had the chance to say goodbye to the boys in this book. People weren't connected like they are today. We didn't have the technology to keep in touch.

We relied on gossip. Acquaintances would cross your path and bring you news. These messengers of death caught you by surprise.

I was standing in the check-out aisle at the Marlee Matlin Von's supermarket when I learned of Rob Kreuger's passing. I was thumbing through an issue of Entertainment Weekly, his name was listed in a column of actors who had died of AIDS.

A flight attendant on layover confirmed the rumors of Duff Paddock's passing. I was floating in the pool of the Hyatt Regency Kaanapali with Camille Darrin. Through AOL I had found her on Maui. A flight attendant in uniform spotted us. It must have been like seeing Rizzo and Kenickie without Sandy and Danny.

"Oh my god! If only Duff and Dean were here!" he screamed across the pool and across the years.

Scott Reader confirmed that Duff had died in his hometown of Sacramento in 1989. Scott was one of Duff's new Hollywood friends, they had worked together at Joe Allen. He told us Dean Frey had met a handsome millionaire and was living with him in homes between Switzerland and Mykonos. As it turned out this was old news.

By this time Dean had passed of AIDS in Europe. This was confirmed by his former landlord, Richard Klug, a Beverly Hills realtor who had crossed paths with Dean and his new lover in the Swiss Alps. Richard Klug owned a legendary apartment tower at the foot of Santa Monica Pier. Not only did Dean live there, but Camille did once, too. Rickie Lee Jones did too, but she had been evicted. There was a framed eviction notice in Camille's apartment. I crossed paths with Richard Klug at Stephen Henderson's funeral.

Stephen Henderson's funeral in Newport Beach was Standing Room Only. The mourners were in high spirits. We were relieved not to be mourning another AIDS death. We were giddy that Stephen died of natural causes: he had been bludgeoned to death by a hustler he picked up at Numbers in West Hollywood. Natural for a homosexual from the 1960s.

Lady Ashtray announced that Stephen's friends on Oahu were doing a paddle out and tossing leis on the ocean. At this funeral I saw Bradley Caine and Len Wrona for the last time.

Michael Rotella died shortly after. His passing was eclipsed by the overdose death of porn star Joey Stefano.

I spent most of these dark days on Ativan. Nights I was drinking alone in dark bars. The tranquilizer Ativan is notorious for causing memory loss.

I tell you this, because my information on Donnie McPhedran has not been confirmed. I think I saw Donnie McPhedran tending bar in Palm Springs, I registered he looked sick, either from AIDS or Meth. Later, I heard bar talk that he had died. All I know that he was lost to AIDS one way or the other.

I lost track of Stevie B. I can only hope he made it out alive.

Hal Story died in San Diego. I was surprised that he has a panel on the AIDS Memorial Quilt.

My remembrance of Hal was published on *The AIDS Memorial* on Instagram. I received a message from a man who said he was Hal's lover at the time he died. He told me that the post had been published on Hal's birthday. I wanted to ask him what the red high-heel signified on Hal's quilt. Was my surfer dream a drag queen?

The AIDS Memorial on Instagram confirmed John from Santa Barbara had died. I wanted to reach out and ask his last name. I did find out the salesman at Neiman's gave him that necktie, I mistakenly assumed that John had stolen it.

Larry Lane died in Cocoa Florida. Mike Tholl told me when he was visiting Bo Frieden. He also told me that Larry's Friends Marty and Alvaro had also died.

Deaths came one after the other like dominoes falling.

Mark McCleary, Grady Wiley, Brad Caine, Len Wrona, Dave Kelley, and James Stonelake all died. Along with my high school boyfriend Jere Timblin

I Will Survive | CHAPTER 36

Twenty years and half a million AIDS deaths later, Bo Frieden dropped back into my life like an astronaut returning from outer space. It was a new millennium, I had finally found that boyfriend I had been searching the country for. Like a deposed dictator, I was living in exile in Manhattan Beach, California.

Laguna Beach and my lost friends was a lifetime ago. That was paradise lost. I had found a new volleyball court. Like an ostrich, I had escaped the AIDS crisis by burying my head in the sand. Literally. Instead of acting up, I hid among married couples playing volleyball in Manhattan Beach. My game had improved playing against firemen and lifeguards. I was now entering competitions along the west coast.

My Florida friend Kevin, found Bo living in a retirement village in Oceanside, CA. Bo had lost his latest fortune and Bobby, but he still had his Billy Haines white velvet sofas. These still had the red wine stains from Judy Garland. Bo was now in his mid-seventies. He still drove a manual shift blue sports car. This one was a Mitsubishi Eclipse.

Now, I was the one burning through a small fortune. I invited Bo up to my beach house for a barbecue party after our annual volleyball tournament. I briefly worried about what tales

Bo would tell my new straight friends as he watched us play volleyball.

Bo captivated all of them, except for my boyfriend, Kris, who volunteered to run to the house for more vodka for Bo's martini.

"Thanks, Bubbie, it's medicinal."

Bo had developed a Parkinson's like tremor in his hands. He believed the alcohol calmed the shaking. It did not. Bo lost most of the alcohol over the edge of the martini glass, like a bartender swirling vermouth.

Kris repeatedly suggested Bo drink ice water.

"I haven't had a sip of water since 1948," Bo boasted, "the Israeli military trained us to go without."

"Humans can't survive without water," Kris said in disbelief. He drank 8 glasses a day. I tried to remember if I had ever seen Bo take a sip of water on all the hot volleyball courts we played on. Kris thought he saw through Bo's tall tales, especially about the Krofft's H.R. Pufnstuf.

"Bo, did you know, Syd Krofft is a good friend of mine." Kris taunted Bo, "let's call him right now!"

Kris was eager to catch Bo in a fib. Soon, Kris was handing his cel phone to Bo, the two septuagenarians spent a half hour laughing outrageously.

I couldn't tell whom Kris was more upset with, Bo, Syd Krofft or me.

"I'm going up to the house to prepare the food so that your guests will have something to eat." I had made it to the finals of the volleyball tournament, my friends would understand why the grill wasn't hot.

I won the tournament. And I finally had the boyfriend I had wanted for so many years.

Kris offered to help Bo back up the hill to our house. Bo's knee had never been replaced. Kris was a compassionate man. Kris kept me up all night bellyaching.

"If I had to listen one more time about the second Mrs. Carrington," he railed.

Kris was an actor and he could make any story hysterical in the telling. "While I'm listening for the sixth time about him flying in the Israeli War of Independence," Kris pauses for dramatic effect, "your friend Bo, is picking off his flaking skin like Goldmember in *Austin Powers*, and flicking it on the purple shag carpeting."

I already knew I'd be vacuuming at dawn.

Kris couldn't dampen the thrill I felt being reconnected with Bo. Bo was proof I didn't just dream my twenties. He was the only man still alive to confirm my stories about Laguna Beach. These were just not an old man's tall tales. Everything really happened as I remembered. We laughed about Flo and the drag queen armada. We were cautious about whom we spoke, the AIDS pandemic was still claiming lives, one was never sure what minefield we were treading on. I brought up Duff, Donnie and Dean, but Bo didn't engage fully. They were my ghosts.

Bo's were ghosts of another era, Judy Garland, Billy Haines and Darko. Bo was happy to report that Dan Downs, Mike Tholl and Ron Rudderow were still among the living.

Kris and I were invited to a 75th birthday party for Bo that Dan's ex-lover Matt Midgett was throwing at their mountain-top mansion in Escondido the next weekend.

"It sounds like *Romy and Michelle's High School Reunion*," Kris declined to join me. "You can play Hansel and Gretel without me. You can follow the trail of Bo's skin flakes and spilt martinis."

My Florida friend Kevin was working in California and Bo invited him with the promise of fixing him up with a hot number.

Like our trip to Fort Lauderdale, I insisted Kevin take his own car. I had just been gifted a candy apple red 1967 Ford Mustang GTA 390.

A dear friend had placed the winning bid in a silent auction for APLA. (AIDS Project Los Angeles had gotten a much-needed contribution and I got an almost brand new 1967 pony car thanks to Amanda Bearse.)

I hand cranked all four windows down—the car was a true hardtop. I was going to take the long way down via Pacific Coast Highway. For the first time in 20 years, now that I found Bo, I felt it was safe to drive through Laguna again. And reminisce. I dug out a disco mixtape that I inherited from a deceased friend. In those dark days there was always a cardboard box filled with belongings one didn't want the parents to see. After the funeral they ended up with me. Stacks of Blue Boy magazines, dozens of Sylvester 12" promotional LPs and enough dildoes to stretch from Laguna to San Francisco when laid end to end.

France Joli blared as I drove down Pacific Coast Highway. From Hermosa Beach through Corona del Mar, everything had changed. Nothing looked familiar, forty years of my life had been bulldozed and rebuilt.

Out of habit, I pulled over in Oceanside to cruise the marines. George W had not yet sent them to the Gulf War. My first stop was the Triple X video arcade. I peered through the glory holes hoping to find a date to take to the party.

This was not uncommon. In the 80's we were always taking strangers to parties. Twenty years before, Steven Henderson was driving his suicide-door Lincoln Continental to a party at Bob Marr's in San Diego. I saw a shirtless boy hitch-hiking at the onramp from Oceanside.

"Let's pick him up."

He was lean and tan and reminded me of Greg Leinart from Daytona Beach. Steve Henderson was always up for mischief.

Before I had introduced myself to my potential boyfriend, Steve had abandoned the driver's seat and jumped in the backseat with the half-naked kid, "Home, James."

I slid over to drive the 1961 Continental.

"Your name is James?" The kid asked excitedly. "My brother's name is James!"

"Young, dumb and full of cum" was an expression we used in the 80's. This kid had to be dumb, hitch-hiking in Oceanside while the Freeway Killer was on the loose, throwing naked Marines along the side of this very same interstate.

"Haven't you watched the news?"

"I don't have a TV. I don't have a place to stay."

"My name is not James, I'm Dave," I introduce myself shaking his dirty hand. "That is Steven Henderson."

"I'm Bob Marr," the kid fends off Steve's wandering hand.

"Bob Marr?" Steve asks incredulously, "We're going to a party thrown by my friend Bob Marr! Come with us."

I can only imagine the mischief Steve is planning.

The real Bob Marr's home is very grand. White marble floors and white silk furniture. The house is filled with hundreds of gay guys who have never met their host. The preppy look has taken over, last year's Polo shirts over Madras shorts. San Diego queens can be so precious. Although flying high on MDA, they conduct themselves as if they are at a Junior League mixer. Their manners are on point.

"Have you met Bob Marr?" Steve pulls one particularly pinched man aside and introduces our homeless friend.

"Thank you so much for having us, your home is fabulous, I adore the grand piano," she gushes confusing the shirtless kid.

"You'll have to come to our house in La Jolla tomorrow for brunch! Chad is making lobster Benedict."

Chad is pulled into the conversation. Chad was posing against the Lucite piano wearing pink trousers and a Madras plaid sport coat over his polo shirt. On the white marble floor his Sperry Topsider boat shoes contrast with the dirty bare feet of his assumed host.

"It will be casual, come as you are."

The kid's bare feet and bare chest are causing tension in this couple. "Biff insists on serving California sparkling wine."

Steven grabs a glass of champagne from a passing waiter. "It's Cristal," he informs Bob Marr who guzzles it greedily.

"If he swallows cock like he swallows champagne, "I overhear Chad remark to Biff, "I can understand how he's come to own this stunning house."

There were no bare-chested marines to wrap in ribbons and bows to take as a present to Bo's party. My vintage Mustang made chatting them up easy. They approached me. They refused my invite. How times had changed. Although serial killers didn't strike fear in a Marine, AIDS did.

June Gloom had blown in, obscuring the canyon that led to Escondido. This fog was thick and cold. I rolled up the hardtop's windows to fight off the chill.

Highway 78 took you into Escondido, a town pockmarked with auto body shops and infested with bikers. I couldn't unwind the Mustang's 390 V8 because I was stuck behind a taco truck. For 10 years we had driven to parties from Malibu to La Jolla, this was the first time I had ever driven to Escondido for a party. It was hard to imagine a grand gay mansion among this hardscrabble community.

Dan and Matt had named their mountaintop aerie "Le Nid De L'aigle" which translates to Eagle's Nest. I had printed the Mapquest map off the computer. A benefit of having the windows rolled up, the pages of directions were not blowing out of my hand. I gunned the Mustang once I turned off 78 and was clear of the Taco truck.

I had to hit the brakes as the road became a series of hairpin turns. The guardrails all looked like they had met Kevin's Monte Carlo. It felt like I was ascending one of those spiral exits in a tier parking garage. Around and around, I went headed to the top of a mountain. A wall of jagged rocks on one side and dented guardrails on the other.

The marine layer was too thick to see what lay beyond the guardrails. In the nick of time, the fog lifted. A pickup truck was bouncing down the hill. Headed straight towards me. I didn't realize this was a two-lane road. I squeezed closer to the guardrail to let the truck pass. Now I could see what lay beyond. The sparkling Pacific Ocean floated miles away. The noon day sun burnt off the fog. Le Nid De L'aigle' was perched alone at the top of this mountain. It truly was an Eagle's Nest.

My heart was beating with excitement. Dozens of shiny sports cars crowded a gravel entry. A valet parker took my Mustang. He was a humpy Mexican kid with an ass like Duffs.

"Señor Matt and Don Dan at the pool," he said in Spanglish. I followed a stone path lined with fragrant rosemary. High above the fog, the sun was as hot as if we were in Palm Springs. I heard raucous laughter coming from beyond the gardens. The pool sounded like West Street Beach twenty years ago.

"Gin!" I recognized a voice from the past. Ron Rudderow must be playing cards. I got all choked up, listening for voices I knew would not hear. As if emerging from the hidden arch to West Street Beach, I saw dozens of familiar faces, though much older now.

Almost 100 gay men were around the pool living, laughing and loving. The pool was carved into a massive stone that lay atop the mountain. This formed a grotto over which a waterfall cascaded. Under which two naked porn stars cavorted.

I recognized them from the stacks of Blue Boy magazines that I had inherited. Their names were Kevin Williams and Lane Fuller.

"David Churchill!" I was lifted off my feet in a bear hug and thrown into the pool by Dan Downs. Instead of getting out and greeting my host, I swam over to the grotto. Kevin Williams introduced himself as Ted. Much more of a man than the twink he was in Blue Boy. He had grown up into a handsome, muscular blue eyed blond, with creamy golden skin. He introduced Lane as his lover. A pink double ended dildo got sucked into the pool filter and caused the waterfall to stop.

"Churchill, what have you done now?" My friend Kevin shouted from across the pool.

I dislodged the dildo from the filter and the waterfall started to pour again. I stood under the waterfall while it cascaded down my bronzed body, finally I was living out my Jennifer Beals fantasy. I thrust the pink dildo triumphantly over my head, like an Oscar winner.

The gallery erupted in applause.

But not for me. Three well-built Texans were traipsing across the waterfall dressed like Esther Williams, they had rubber bathing caps and one-piece swimsuits.

I realized I was in the midst of the afternoon's entertainment. As an Occasional Man from South Pacific wafted out of speakers disguised as rocks, the bathing beauties began a synchronized swim routine, high-kicking while they floated on their backs linked like a daisy, all the while the porn stars teeter-tottered on the pink dildo in time to the music.

Mexican houseboys surreptitiously removed ashtrays, their eyes averted from the decadent spectacle. One particularly cute one brought me an ice-cold Margarita.

"Gracias, amigo."

With this liquid courage, I dared to sit down at the card table. Coming of age with these men I had been scolded many times for chatting while they were playing bridge. Now, twenty years later it was enough to just sit silently among the living.

Ron Rudderow now had a young boyfriend. Reggie Feuille was an excellent bridge partner, and he could play volleyball. Ron was turning beet red because Bo and Dan Downs were telling a colorful story with no end in sight. Coming in late, I gleaned they were talking about securing seed money for the launch of NTN.

Between the guffaws and back slapping, the plot seemed lifted from a Scorsese movie. There were Italian Restaurants and Coupe De Villes. At first it seemed like another one of Bo's Tall Tales. Until Dan Downs introduced details like a Halliburton case full of cash, that seemed to validate Bo's story. They survived the machine gun assault on the Coupe De Ville and ended up with the suitcase of cash.

These men were the father figures I never had. They taught me how to play volleyball. They taught me how to entertain. They taught me the morals that were valued in gay life. I knew which utensil to use with which course. I knew which side my bread was buttered on. I had managed to land a humpy number to be my boyfriend.

I wish Kris were here so I could show these men how well I had done.

Ron Rudderow slammed his hand down on the bridge table. Queens screamed around the pool and jumped up from their chaise lounges. Car alarms rang from the parking lot. To me it felt like Ron had triggered the earthquake. It was just another California tremor.

"Let's play volleyball instead of bridge," Dan declared.

Ron Rudderow seemed temporarily soothed by the suggestion. "But we are miles from the beach, on top of a mountain."

"Trust you to state the obvious, Churchill." At forty, I was still a pedantic twenty-year old.

Bo had once taken me aside and advised that I be less literal and more imaginative, "You'll be happier, Bubbie!"

Besides Ron, Reggie, Bo and Myself, Dan had begun rounding up volleyball players. He pried Matt away from supervising the caterers in the kitchen.

We followed another winding garden path, giant stones were placed as benches to take in the sunset views to the west over the ocean. Le Nid De L'aigle was the only home on the top of this mountain. The three Texas bathing beauties had joined the parade.

"Where are we going?" They asked.

"To play volleyball!" Dan answered just as the path opened to a sand volleyball court perched on a ridge of the mountain.

"How did you do this?" I gasped at this mirage.

A two-story tall screen fence surrounded the sand volleyball court to keep the ball from going over the edge of the mountain, like Hal's San Diego queens at Deep Creek. The Pacific Ocean sparkled beyond the screen.

This had to be heaven.

As if 20 years had never passed, Bo, Dan, Ron and I were back on a sand volleyball court.

Two of the Texan bathing beauties tore off their rubber bathing caps and joined us on the court. The drunkest of the Texans sat on the sidelines cheering us on. Matt Midgett and Reggie Feuille brought us to ten, we divided into teams of five.

Bo drew a circle in the sand around him, "Don't make me move from this circle. Pass the ball into the circle and I will score the point!"

This triggered the Texas queen to draw the Olympic circles on the other team's side, In her giddiness, the drunk one fell down and made snow angels in the sand.

I stayed in touch with Bo Frieden until the day he died. Living alone on Social Security, he mastered the new technology of the World Wide Web. He was scouring the chatrooms searching for the next Mrs. Frieden. He took his daily walk past the boats in the Oceanside Marina to the volleyball court at the pier, where he sometimes played.

"You've got to come down and play. I play with the hottest number since Darko, he's 16 and he's kept by a country superstar."

The advent of cell phones made it easier to stay in touch. You kept the same phone number no matter where you moved. I had lost touch with most of my old friends, my address book had multiple area codes crossed out-714 beget 760 and eventually became 949. Bo had sold most of the Billy Haines furniture on eBay when he moved into his Section 8 housing. He never regained his fortunes, but it didn't seem to matter to him. Even with his bum knee, he still drove his manual shift Mitsubishi Eclipse like it was a Lotus Europa.

"Bo! You're 80. That doesn't mean the speed limit is." I'd plead.

By now both of his hands had a tremor. I watched the one on the gearshift shake as he downshifted to squeeze between a minivan and a semi. He drove like he was still flying a B-29 bomber.

Bo was telling the truth about the 16-year-old volleyball player. Bo and I challenged him and his dad. The kid was beautiful and he oozed confidence and charisma. We shook hands under the net before we began our game.

"I'm Andrew Keegan," he introduced himself making eye contact. I had seen that name linked with country superstar LeeAnn Rimes on the internet. Once again, Bo's story holds true.

"Churchill. I've found the next Mrs. Frieden." Bo pulls me aside and whispers to me, "I walk into the marina restroom and find this 13-year-old boy hiding behind a 13-inch dick."

I'm familiar with that restroom having cruised for Marines there. In an attempt to mitigate the lewd and lascivious conduct, the city of Oceanside had removed the stall doors so that you have to sit without privacy. Embarrassing if you want to do your business, but great advertising if you are there to cruise. I can vividly picture Bo's description of this kid. The first thing you would notice is the erection, then the kid behind it.

Bo's last days were spent in home hospice, his Medicare plan provided a 24-hour caregiver.

"I didn't get a hot number. I've got a girl, Melissa. She's got tattoos." Bo sounds disappointed.

By the time I got down to say goodbye he and Melissa were thick as thieves. Bo slips me an Oxycodone. He is high on morphine. Bo retells his greatest hits. Flying B-29s in the Israeli war of Independence.

Hearing these another time, Melissa cocks her eyebrow as if asking me, "Is this True?"

I cannot confirm that everything really happened as Bo tells it. Thanks to my boyfriend Kris, I do know the Hemisfair68 story is true. Bo Frieden indeed brought Sid & Mary Krofft aboard to create the puppet mascot that later became H. R. Pufnstuf.

Bo runs out of steam, "Dan built a sand volleyball court on top of a mountain, and we all played volleyball together one last time. It was like being in heaven. My team won."

It's true. We did win.

Bo wanted his ashes scattered on the volleyball court at Oceanside.

Bo Frieden was the first friend to die of a long life well lived, I was able to prepare a proper goodbye. I collected a bucket of sand from the volleyball court at West Street Beach, where Bo said he sunk the poles some forty years before. A bartender in Key West had Fed-Exed me some sand from the volleyball court Bo had played on in the 1960's. I mixed those with his ashes, I thought it made a fitting send off.

Through tears, I started the long drive home alone, I stopped to pee at the Marina restroom.

"Hey Mister," I hear a boy's voice crack.

I turn around to see a teenager exposing himself in the doorless stall.

"A 13-year-old boy hiding behind a 13-inch dick." Bo was telling the truth! This was like finding out Santa Claus was real. Bo wasn't exaggerating. The kid had to be 13 and his dick was bigger than he was.

I called Melissa the caregiver, "*It's Twue, It's twue!*" This sighting confirmed every story Bo ever told was true.

You don't need to run into a teenager in a public restroom to confirm my stories are true. You can find our initials on the cars at Cadillac Ranch.

Three of the boys in this book survived the AIDS pandemic, and we are still friends. Bucky, MJ, and Kevin Crew can confirm these stories are true.

Duff, Dean, Donnie, John, Michael, Larry and Hal once walked beside me and made me the man I am today.

Author | D. David Churchill

A native Californian, I was raised by a single mother in the Rust Belt. I spent my life trying to fit in. My only ambition was to be tan and blonde.

Upon high school graduation, I returned to California to reclaim my birthright and attend college. I lived at the beach. I was Seal Beach Dave. I was Church in Laguna Beach and West Hollywood. On the volleyball courts in Manhattan Beach, I was Hollywood Dave—a wink to my homosexuality.

In retirement, I am a nomad who lives in an Airstream Travel Trailer, usually at the beach. I no longer try to fit in. This is my first book. I left family and friends to unplug and focus on writing this book. Because there is already a published author named David Churchill, a novelist from Britain, I've chosen to publish under a new name. D. David Churchill.

Photo Credit: Ronnie Todd

I'm currently in Florida where I have been nicknamed "Daiquiri" Dave. At 65, I am still tan and blonde.